Charlie &

One-act theatr

Tina O Rour

Published by Clockworkarts Publishing
Galway, Ireland.

First published 2007
Second edition 2024

ISBN 978-0-9553383-4-2

Dedication

To Margaret Fitzpatrick
always remembered & sadly missed.

To my Dad, who supported all of my creative pursuits
no matter how crazy they were.
I will miss you forever.

Introduction

I wrote this play in the spring of 1999, and it went into production in June of the same year, debuting in Galway before going on a micro tour to the Dublin Fringe Festival in the autumn.

The piece is character-driven and explores Charlie and Nora's experience growing up in Ireland during the 50s and 60s before entering a new world as Ireland prepared to transition to the noughties.

I developed the script, Charlie & Nora, intending to maintain the nostalgia of a former world and the people it created, juxtaposed with the newly emerging internet and the many worldwide connecting social structures that were yet to come.

Viewing the piece now in 2024 affords me an interesting introspection. I now live in a time where people's truth and their hidden shame have simultaneously become public and remained hidden. Where ideas and ideologies polarize societies and voices of opinion overwhelm them.

Re-reading my script, I believe it is a piece of its time. Everyone's journey is as individual to them as they express themselves. Charlie and Nora are two humans exploring their connection in their present through a lens of their past. Two individuals connect, share, and ultimately accept each other's truth without judgment.

Tina, January 2024

Charlie & Nora

First presented in Ireland at the Town Hall Theatre,
Galway, Ireland on the 7th June 1999
with the following cast:

CHARACTERS

Charlie - Ger Considine
Nora - Bernie Guinane

Scene:
The action takes place in an
inner city park late in the evening.

There is an old wooden bench centre stage. Next to the bench is a tall streetlight. It is the middle of the night and the light from the streetlight diffuses a soft warm glow on the bench. It is an overcast night, but dry and not too cold. In the distance the sound of an active city hums in the background.

For the first thirty seconds the sound is loud, then over the following thirty seconds it starts to fade out until it is a slight hum in the background.

Then for a further thirty seconds we can only hear the hum of the city in the far off distance and the silence surrounding the bench. Suddenly there is the sound of a couple laughing heartily from stage left.

Charlie 'O' she doth teach the torches to burn bright!
Her beauty hangs upon the cheek of the night'.

Enter Charlie and Nora from stage left. They are both in their mid fifties. Charlie is wearing a long overcoat and his hair is neatly combed into a side parting.

He is neat and carries himself well. Nora is dressed in an eclectic and eccentric manner. She wears all her hair up under a large floppy peaked hat and carries a large brown bag. It has the look of a bag that contains a woman's life.

Nora And you say he has only just met her!

Charlie 'fraid so.

Nora Foolish, foolish boy. Sure it will never work.

Charlie Will you stop trying to jump ahead in my story? Now, where was I?

Nora Night.

Charlie Oh yes, I remember now, he waffles a bit more about the same stuff and then says, 'did my heart love till now? Foreswear it, sight! For I ne'er saw true beauty till this night'.

Nora		See I told you.

Charlie		What?

Charlie makes an elaborate seating gesture towards Nora.

Charlie		Well your ladyship, shall we sit?

Nora		I don't see why not!

Nora sits down first and places her bag on her lap. Charlie straightens his coat and sits down next to her. They sit in silence for a few seconds. Charlie is breathing in and out serenely. Nora is looking around slowly at the view. There isn't much to see so she gets bored pretty quickly.

Nora		So, aren't you going to finish the story?

(Looking at Nora)

Nora		(Smiling) Aren't you?

Charlie		Would you like me to?

Nora		Of course I would.

Charlie		Are you sure it's not really because you're bored?

Nora		I'm not bored, not at all. (Lying)

Charlie		Mmh, I thought so. 'For tis in vain to seek him here that means not to be found'.

Nora		What nonsense is that?

Charlie		'He jests at scars that never felt a wound'.

Nora		Look now, stop this nonsense and continue with the story.

Charlie		I am.

Nora Well, I never heard anyone speak those lines in the film.

Charlie What film?

Nora The film of the story you are telling me.

Charlie But I thought you didn't know the story?

Nora Arra sure I do!

Charlie But all of those lines that I've quoted are in the play, even the ones I said earlier. I thought you knew I was telling you about a play.

Nora No... Sure I was only humouring you back then.

Charlie Humouring me?

Nora Sure I thought you had made them up. I didn't know there was a play based on the film.

Charlie (Frowns) The film is based on the play.

Nora So you know the film.

Charlie Of course I do, everyone knows Westside Story is based on Romeo and Juliet.

Nora Really?

Charlie Yes, really.

Charlie straightens himself up and sits stiffly. There is a short silence.

Nora But sure I think your words are far more romantic than the ones in the film.

Charlie Do you think so?

Nora Positively.

Charlie There is only one problem.

Nora And what's that?

Charlie They're not my words.

Nora No?

Charlie Afraid so, they're Shakespeare's.

Nora Arra get away outa that.

Charlie No, it's true.

Nora He sounds like he's a right romantic auld chap.

Charlie So you like his words then?

Nora Arra sure, I do.

Charlie Oh, that's just great Nora.

Nora Now mind you though, I still think he's foolish. Falling for a young one and all he has done has seen her.

Charlie But that's the romance of it.

Nora That's the stupidity of it.

Charlie But...

Nora And as I have said, it will all come to wrong in the end. I've seen the film and I know. All that because of a pretty looking girl.

Charlie But Nora, it's only a story.

Nora Sure I know that, but what else do I have to get excited about?

Charlie I know, but you know while you're here you are lady over all you can see.

Nora Charlie, there's not a lot for seeing here.

Charlie Oh, but there is.

Nora It's just a cold bench, in a cold park, on a winter's night.

Charlie It may be that, but to me it is something far more.

Nora How Charlie?

Charlie Did you know I was born near here?

Nora No, I thought you were from out the country.

Charlie That's true, but I started here.

Nora I started here myself, not that it's much to talk about.

Charlie I know the feeling.

Silence.

Charlie I still haven't explained to you why I call this my silent place.

Nora You will.

Charlie stands up and walks over to the streetlight. He looks up into the light and as he does it flickers.

Charlie (He points to the light) that's what they are like my memories.

Nora (Amused) like a streetlight?

Charlie No, like flickers of light; a slow motion film in segments.

Nora Segments?

Charlie	Pieces, sections, small bits, but never the complete picture.
Nora	It takes other people to make up the full picture, you know.
Charlie	Only too well.
Nora	So, what are these memories like?
Charlie	Like I've said, like parts of old films, you know silent films.
Nora	Is that why you call this your silent place?
Charlie	I wish, no, I may not be able to hear in my memories but I sure as hell can feel. There is no silence where volcanoes erupt.
Nora	How do you mean?
Charlie	Memories hurt, even silent ones.
Nora	Not all memories are bad Charlie.

Charlie smiles at Nora and sits back down. Nora starts to root through her bag. After rummaging for a bit she pulls out a photograph.

Nora	See. (She shows the photograph to Charlie) I remember when he was born.
Charlie	Who is he?
Nora	My grandson.
Charlie	You're not a grandmother?
Nora	I am.
Charlie	Nora, you astound me.

Nora	I was very happy when he was born. He is such a lovely little chap.
Charlie	(Taking the photograph) How old is he?
Nora	He's two, just gone, born on the 14th October.
Charlie	Almost a Halloween baby.
Nora	Almost.
Charlie	So what's it like to be a grandmother? (He hands her back the photograph)
Nora	Normal, the only thing that's different is, I can't run after him all that quick. It makes me realise how old I've gotten.
Charlie	You're not old Nora.
Nora	No, just a bit creaky.

Charlie laughs.

Nora	The only thing that's strange is my baby having a baby.
Charlie	Is it your daughter's child?
Nora	Oh no, she's not interested in babies at all; he's my son's baby.
Charlie	(Joking) Oh, a bit of a mammy's boy is he?
Nora	No, not at all.
Charlie	I bet you still cook some dinners for him.
Nora	No I don't. Only the odd time. Well, I have to now.
Charlie	Why?

Nora He's by himself and he works a lot.

Charlie Oh.

Nora Oh, it's not bad, it just didn't work out.

Charlie Married were they?

Nora Not at all, sure you know the young ones of today.

Charlie I do.

Nora You'd never have had that in our time.

Charlie Yes you did.

Nora Not the way I was raised, you didn't.

Charlie You even had it in our parents' time, Nora.

Nora Well, I wouldn't know about that.

Charlie I do. My father made off when I was a baby, and my mother couldn't cope so I went to live with me aunt. That's why everyone thought I was from the country. I was born right next door to the house I live in now. Just like the

Charlie Salmon I say, we will always come back to the place of our birth. Nora, am I boring you?

Nora No.

Charlie Is there anything wrong?

Nora I think we had best be getting home.

Charlie So soon?

Nora I'm cold.

Charlie starts to undo his overcoat.

Charlie Well, you can have my overcoat if you like.

Nora No, we must go now.

Charlie Listen Nora, what is wrong?

Nora (Angrily) Nothing, just nothing.

Silence.

Nora Well they were married, weren't they?

Charlie Who?

Nora Your parents.

Charlie Yes, but...

Nora See, it didn't happen back then.

Charlie But, Nora it's just as bad if your parents were married or not.

Nora No, it isn't.

Charlie Don't be silly Nora, being without your parents, whether they were married or not, is tough on any child.

Nora I'm not being silly.

Nora gets up to leave.

Charlie Why do you have to be so embarrassed that your son isn't married?

Nora I'm not.

Charlie Yes you are.

Nora No Charlie, I'm embarrassed because my mum wasn't married.

Nora sits back down on the bench and Charlie walks to the side of the bench. Silence.

Charlie — I'm sorry.

Nora — It's ok, it's out now.

Charlie — I didn't mean to.

Nora — I know.

Charlie — You know you don't have to be embarrassed.

Nora — Oh yes Charlie, I do.

Charlie — Nora, I remember how it felt when I was a child, not having any parents around. Me aunt was great, but...

Nora — But still she was family Charlie.

Charlie — I know that, look Nora what can I say?

Nora — Nothing Charlie, nothing.

Silence.

Nora — Do you know what the word illegitimate means?

Charlie — Yes, I do know what it means. Why?

Nora — No Charlie, do you really know what it means?

Charlie — Born outside of wedlock, but that doesn't really matter any more, it never really mattered.

Nora — Jesus Charlie, yes it did.

Charlie looks at Nora. He takes her hand in his.

Charlie — Nora?

Nora		What Charlie?

Charlie		You know it doesn't matter to me.

Nora		But that's just it Charlie, it doesn't matter to you, it matters to me.

Nora slowly takes her hand back out of Charlie's hand. Silence.

Nora		You know, I used to have to mind all the babies as they arrived. It's what the nuns thought I was good at.

Charlie		Nuns Nora? Where you in a convent?

Nora		No Charlie, an orphanage run by nuns.

Charlie		Oh!

Silence.

Nora		Now do you understand Charlie?

Charlie		Sometimes Nora I'm just really stupid, all the sight in the world and I can't see what's under my nose.

Nora		Not an awful lot of people can.

Nora smiles.

Charlie		I suppose Shakespeare doesn't get us very far out here.

Nora		No Charlie, not out here.

Charlie smiles at Nora. Silence.

Nora		Now you see, it's not my son, it's me. Still you're right though, it would have been nice if he was married.

Charlie Do you think so?

Nora Well, it's a bit selfish but I'd have liked to have seen them have the big wedding, you know the white dress and everything.

Charlie Yes, but now they'd be getting divorced.

Nora Oh, yea, I don't know much how I'd feel about that.

Charlie Lack of thought and commitment is how I feel about it.

Nora There wasn't much thought in our day either Charlie. It was just the done thing.

Charlie (Wistfully) Yea.

Silence.

Charlie So tell me, does it really bother you that much today?

Nora What?

Charlie Being brought up in an orphanage.

Nora Yea, it does you know. It's not so much that people care today, particularly not with how everything is opening up with the church. It's funny, they now think we're the victims, but we didn't know any different at the time. People don't really understand the stigma attached to us back then, but once you've felt it you will always carry it (taps at her heart) in here.

Charlie Is it that bad?

Nora Not really Charlie, It's just a way of life and you learn to live with it and try your best to avoid talking about the subject.

Charlie Not succeeding very well are you?

Nora (Smiles) No. You know I never really spoke about it, not until I had me own kids. Then you couldn't stopme. The kids loved to hear stories about the nuns and all the mischief I used to get up to. It was like I'd take them on a great adventure every time I told them a story.

Charlie Their heroine.

Nora Oh, I don't know about that, more like their own Oliver Twist. The one they loved to hear the most was how I used to sneak down to the pantry and hide in one of the presses that was stuffed with homemade jam. Oh, I used to love the homemade jam, it was the closest thing we had to sweets at the time. I 'd just sit there and eat and eat. I had only done this a few times, particularly on Sundays because it was quiet and you didn't have any chores, when I got caught. 'Nora' she said, she frightened the life out of me, and I knew I was for it. The punishment back then, if you did anything bold, was to cut all you hair off, and they always had a scissors handy deep in the pockets of their big black habits. Well I decided I was having none of it, I hadn't been caught for being bad for quite a while so my hair was pretty long. I also knew the nuns couldn't run very fast in their long frocks so I jumped out of the press, ducked underneath her and ran out the door. She turned like a devil and started to run after me, but she just kept sliding on the shiny wooden floor, the one we had to polish every week. I had just reached the top of the staircase as she was almost about to catch me, but she missed and went flying down the stairs. But as luck has it she was ok. The only thing that happened was the scissors went into her knee. Serves them right for carrying their scissors in

Nora — their long pockets.

Charlie — And was she ok?

Nora — She was fine; she just had a bit of a limp.

Charlie — And what about you?

Nora — They cut off my hair, I didn't tell the children that bit, but that was their favourite story now for ya. I actually used to enjoy telling them the story, I can still see the excitement in their eyes, and it was funny when they used to run around the house one pretending to be me and the other the nun. Kids are so funny at times.

Charlie — I'd love to have had kids.

Nora — Yea, kids are great.

Charlie — (Sadly) Yea.

Nora — They also got to meet their Grandmother.

Charlie — So you knew your mother.

Nora — I suppose you could say that. I met her once when I was a child, on my first communion and then when you reached sixteen you went and joined your mother in the laundry. I wouldn't even speak to her then, I hated her so much. But then again I suppose you mellow as you get older, then after I had my kids I saw her a couple of times before she died and everything was ok. My last memory is of her wearing old plastic bags over her boots, it was snowing you see and it was to keep them dry, she gave the kids ten pence each and I gave her a hug good bye. I never saw her again.

Charlie — I never saw my mother, she went insane after my father left her and she killed herself. My aunt never spoke about her.

Nora looks at Charlie.

Nora — I'm sorry Charlie, I'm really, really sorry.

Charlie — Me too.

Charlie stands up and walks over to the streetlight. Silence.

Charlie — You know, you should have told me you knew the story I was telling you.

Nora looks at him puzzled.

Charlie — You know, Romeo and Juliet.

Nora — (Joking) Arra sure, I had to let you have something to talk about.

Charlie — (Smiles) Sure.

They smile at each other; Nora gets up and walks over to the streetlight. She stares up at it.

Nora — So Charlie, why do you find this streetlight so interesting?

Charlie — You know, I'm not sure.

Nora — Arra, go on outa that, you don't get to our age without knowing why we do things.

Charlie — Some people do.

Nora — You're not just some people though, are you Charlie?

Charlie — Neither are you Nora. You know, there is one thing I do see when I stand here and look up,

Charlie but it's not a memory; it's more of a dream.

Nora Well?

Charlie I'm not so sure I should tell you.

Nora After all I just told you. (Joking) The cheek of ya.

Charlie Well, I suppose I should tell you then.

Nora No supposing in it.

Charlie As long as you promise not to laugh or say I'm silly

Nora Of course I won't.

Charlie Promise.

Nora I promise.

Charlie Are you sure?

Nora Positively.

Charlie Ok then, you see when I was a teenager I never really fitted in. You know, the awkward stage, well my awkward stage lasted most of my life and when I used to go to dances.

Nora Dances?

Charlie Yes dances, you know the ballroom of romance type of thing.

Nora Oh, I know them all right Charlie.

Charlie Didn't you go to them?

Nora Once or twice.

Charlie Is that all? You weren't still in the laundry then?

Nora Oh no, I was out in the early sixties.

Charlie So, how come you only went once or twice?

Nora Well, I went to England.

Charlie Straight away?

Nora Oh no, after a couple of years.

Charlie Didn't you go out?

Nora Oh yes, I liked going out.

Charlie So how come you didn't go to the dances?

Nora Well, you know the stories, don't you Charlie?

Charlie No.

Nora You know, about the girl in Sea point, and it wasn't just there it was all across the country.

Charlie What Nora?

Nora Well you see, there was this young girl who was asked to dance by this handsome gentleman, so she said yes and they spent the entire evening dancing. All of her friends were jealous of her, and just as the evening was about to finish he bent over to give her a kiss, she was a shy sort of a girl so she tilted her head down, and just as she did, didn't she notice that the man she was dancing with had no feet, only two big black hoofs. So that's why I didn't go to many dances, I was too afraid to dance with anyone. You know they said it was the devil.

Charlie Ah Nora, you didn't really believe that?

Nora I did at the time Charlie.

Charlie Well, maybe that's why no one danced with me.

Nora Ah, don't be silly Charlie. The only thing I can't believe is that you never heard the story.

Charlie Oh, I did, it's just I never paid much attention to it. It was just a story the church cooked up.

Nora You must have been brave then Charlie.

Charlie No, just different.

Nora So are you ever going to tell me?

Charlie What?

Nora About your dream.

Charlie Oh yes, you see I used to go to the dances but I never actually had the courage to ask any one out so before I got there I used to imagine I was... now promise you won't laugh.

Nora I won't. So who?

Charlie Dean Martin.

Nora has to hold in a giggle.

Charlie See I told you.

Nora I'm not laughing Charlie. (Trying to hold it in)

Charlie No, but you want to.

Nora I don't, I don't, it's just, well...

Charlie looks at her.

Nora All the other boys wanted, was to get a kiss and

Nora — a cuddle of us girls and all you wanted to do was croon to your girl.

Charlie — All I wanted to do was have a dance.

Nora — Yes, but you have to admit it Dean Martin did a lot more crooning that necking in his films.

Charlie — Maybe.

Nora — Charlie what's this leading to?

Charlie — Well, I suppose it was the long way round to ask you. But, what I'd like to say is, will you dance with me Nora?

Nora — Dance with you?

Charlie — Yes.

Nora — Where?

Charlie — Here?

Nora — Oh no.

Charlie — Why?

Nora — Because we're outside.

Charlie — If you mean, it's because people will see us, well they won't because there is no one around.

Nora — Oh, I don't know Charlie.

Charlie — You can even check my feet first.

Nora — I won't need to do that now, will I?

Charlie — Well?

Nora — I can't really dance with out music.

Charlie But we have music Nora.

Nora Where?

Charlie It's all around us.

Nora All I can hear is the city in the distance.

Charlie It's there too, but you have to listen carefully.

Nora Ah Charlie, don't be silly.

Charlie See I told you, you'd say I was silly.

Nora But this is silly.

Charlie You'll be breaking your promise if you don't at least give me a chance to show you.

Nora You tricked me.

Charlie No I didn't, I just want to share something with you.

Nora Ok, what do I have to do?

Charlie Nothing, the sound will find you when you stop looking for it.

Nora I don't understand what you mean.

Charlie Ok, we'll make it easier, just sit down comfortably. (Nora sits and Charlie sits next to her) Now close your eyes. (Charlie runs his hands over her eyes to close them) and listen to the silence. Nora opens her eyes and looks at Charlie.

Nora I can't hear anything Charlie.

Charlie I know Nora, but you will, trust me.

Nora		Ok, but it's easier to listen to the sound of the city.

Charlie		Well listen to it then.

Nora closes her eyes again. Charlie takes hold of her hand and bends over to whispers something in her ear. Nora smiles and suddenly we can hear the faint hum of music coming from the city. Charlie holds Nora's hands tightly. The music starts to increase until it fills the stage and the city sounds have disappeared. Nora opens her eyes and looks excitedly at Charlie.

Nora		Charlie, I can...

Charlie puts his finger to her lips and then stands up. He gestures for her to dance with him. Nora holds her head coyly and holds out her hand. They dance together under the streetlight. Charlie holds her head delicately. Nora has her head on his shoulder. They dance for a while and then Nora raises her head and kisses Charlie on the cheek. This startles Charlie and he jumps back. The music stops and the sound of the city in the distance can be heard again. Nora stands looking at Charlie.

Charlie		I'm sorry.

Nora		I didn't mean to...

Charlie		It's ok.

Nora		I'm a free woman you know Charlie.

Charlie		Look you're not, and for Christ sake will you stop saying my name.

Nora		I'm not Charlie.

Charlie		Yes you are. (He turns away from her) Why do you have to keep saying my name? (Angrily)

Nora turns away shocked, puts her head in her hands and starts to cry.

Charlie	(Turns to face Nora) Oh Nora, don't do this to me, just don't do this to me.
Nora	(Annoyed) Do what Charlie? Show you some affection and talk to you? Is there something wrong with that Charlie? What's so wrong with it Charlie? You're just like him. No, you're worse you open all the right doors and then slam them in my face. Why do you do that Charlie? Why?

Charlie sits down.

Charlie	Please stop saying my name.
Nora	How can I?
Charlie	I hate my name Nora; you don't know how much I hate it.
Nora	Why did you bring me here?
Charlie	To talk to you Nora.
Nora	But why?
Charlie	Because I care about you.
Nora	But Charlie I care about you, that's all I was showing you.
Charlie	I don't want to know it that way Nora.
Nora	Why Charlie? I don't understand.
Charlie	Because that's the way it is.
Nora	That's just what he says, that's the way it is, so you just have to accept it. I don't want to

Nora	accept it, not anymore. I do love him you know, Charlie.
Charlie	I know you do Nora.
Nora	Then you know how hard it is for me to be here with you.
Charlie	But Nora I didn't mean it that way.
Nora	Well what way did you mean it?

No answer.

Nora	(Angrily) Charlie, what way did you mean it?

No answer.

Nora	You see you are the same, when it comes to the crunch you ignore me. The same way he does. Just sits in the couch and ignores me. All I want to do is have him talk to me. That's all, it's not much.
Charlie	I'm not the same as your husband Nora.
Nora	Oh, so now you're listening to me.
Charlie	I never stopped listening to you.
Nora	No?
Charlie	No Nora, I haven't. But there is one thing I have to know.
Nora	What?
Charlie	That's it Nora, what? What do you want?
Nora	I just want to be happy; my life has been bad enough without knowing it is going to be the same when I'm old.

Charlie	I know that Nora, but what is it you really want?
Nora	Peace Charlie, that's all I want, is some peace. You know, to be able to sit in the sitting room watching television, not being ignored. To have someone to go for walks with me and the odd time to go to the pub for a drink.
Charlie	And?
Nora	And maybe the odd hug now and then.
Charlie	You know Nora that's not a lot to ask for.
Nora	I know Charlie.
Silence.	
Nora	We get on, don't we Charlie?
Charlie	I'd like to think so.
Nora	Then why can't...?
Charlie	No Nora.
Nora	Is it because I'm married?
Charlie	No.
Nora	You know I'm not happy there. You know that Charlie don't you?
Charlie	I do.
Nora	You know, Charlie I can move with the times, I see all the young ones today, when they're not happy they can leave. No one says anything today. People would understand. No one would be mad at you being with a married woman.

Charlie That's not the point Nora.

Nora But it is Charlie, you even said it yourself earlier, it doesn't matter to day. It did matter but it doesn't matter any more.

Charlie I don't want us to be that way Nora.

Nora All I want is for us to care for each other.

Charlie I want that too, but it can't be the way you want it to be.

Nora Why Charlie?

Charlie Because that's the way it is.

Nora Is it Charlie, is that the way it really is?

Charlie Yes.

Nora Is that why you never married Charlie?

Charlie What?

Nora Because you couldn't commit.

Charlie No.

Nora You know that's what they say about you.

Charlie Who?

Nora Our group that meets.

Charlie What group?

Nora The bingo group.

Charlie What do they say Nora?

Nora That you lead women up the garden path and

Nora then you run away from them when it gets too serious.

Charlie That's not true.

Nora It is from where I'm standing Charlie. They warned me not to meet you for a drink, 'don't trust him' they said. But I thought you had such a nice face Charlie. I didn't believe them, but now I know I was wrong.

Charlie Nora, please let me explain.

Nora Why should I?

Charlie All I want is for you to be my friend.

Nora And that's it?

Charlie Yes that's it. A friend.

Nora You see I was right, you can't commit.

Charlie But I can, I can commit to being your friend.

Nora What sort of nonsense is that?

Charlie It's not nonsense.

Nora It is with the way you talk, saying that you would have liked to have had children.

Charlie But I would have liked to have had children.

Nora How could you have had Charlie? You couldn't commit to anyone long enough. I'd even wonder if you could commit to your children.

Charlie Nora, please don't say that.

Nora What? That you couldn't have cared for your children if you'd have had any.

Charlie	How could you be so cruel Nora?

Nora	I'm not the one being cruel here Charlie.

Charlie	Yes you are.

Nora	Oh, I've had enough of this. I'm leaving, goodbye Charlie.

Charlie	Nora, please don't go.

Nora	No Charlie, good-bye.

Nora starts to walk away. Charlie stands up trying to contain what he has to say.

Charlie	(Shouts) Nora please. (No answer.) You don't understand. (No answer.) I'm gay.

Nora stands still. Silence. Nora turns around and walks back over to the bench slowly. She sits down. All the time Charlie is looking at her intently for some sort of a reaction, but there is none. Nora then looks up at him.

Nora	I don't understand.

Charlie sits down next to her. Nora moves away from him slightly.

Charlie	I'm gay.

Nora	No, not about that, about all of this.

Charlie	Now, I don't understand.

Nora	This game you're playing with me.

Charlie	I was never playing a game with you.

Nora	Yes you were, you were never interested in me.

Charlie	But, Nora I am interested in you.

Nora How could you be, you just told me you're...

(She nods at him)

Charlie I am gay, but that doesn't mean I can't like you, Nora.

Nora Oh, yes it does.

Nora pulls her bag in closer to her and sits very stiffly.

Charlie You're uncomfortable.

Nora No, I'm not.

Charlie Look Nora, I can tell by the way you are sitting.

Nora It's just I've never been around anyone like that.

Charlie Like what?

Nora You.

Charlie I'm still me.

Nora No, you're not.

Charlie How am I different Nora?

Nora Well, you're not the same person that I knew.

Charlie So who is the person that you knew?

Nora Well he was polite.

Charlie Same.

Nora Kind.

Charlie Same.

Nora	Interesting.
Charlie	Same.
Nora	(Annoyed) Good at listening.
Charlie	Same.
Nora	(Angrily) No, you're not.
Charlie	Yes I am, and I've just discovered that you're the same.
Nora	Of course I am.
Charlie	Yes, the same as all of the other self-centred, bigoted people I know.
Nora	I am not.
Charlie	Oh, yes you are. You were only interested in me because I listened to you.
Nora	That's not true.
Charlie	Then, why was it? Because maybe we could have become intimate and then you would have an excuse to leave your husband?
Nora	How dare you!
Charlie	No Nora, how dare you.
Nora	What?
Charlie	How dare you only like me when it's convenient to you!

Nora looks at him stunned.

Charlie	How dare you expect me to listen to all your stories and accept them when you won't accept

Charlie mine?

Nora stands up to walk away.

Charlie But most of all, how dare you to expect me to care for you unconditionally when you won't for me.

Nora (Angrily) I don't expect you to care for me.

Charlie (Angrily) Then what do you expect.

Nora (Angrily) All I really wanted, was for us to be friends.

They both stop still and look at each other. Silence. Nora sits back down deep in thought and Charlie walks over to the streetlight.

Charlie That's all I wanted.

Nora I know. I haven't really been fair have I?

Charlie No, not really, but you know...

Nora Please... It's just... Well, you see, I'm a bit afraid.

Charlie Of what?

Nora You... No... Of what you are.

Charlie Nora, I'm afraid too. Afraid that people won't accept me for who I am. Of being lonely for the rest of my life. Of waking up every morning and wondering if people are going to be able to see who I really am and not being given a chance to defend myself.

Nora You mean no one knows?

Charlie No.

Nora Why not?

Charlie Well, look at the way you just reacted.

Nora Not your family, your Aunt, no one.

Charlie No, no one except you.

Nora But Charlie, it's the done thing today I see it on the T.V. all the time.

Charlie But, it wasn't when I was younger Nora. You even said that about yourself earlier.

Nora It's not really the same though is it?

Charlie I suppose, but the stigma is the same, Nora.

Nora Well, then why didn't you leave? Even I left Charlie.

Charlie I did try to Nora. I remember I used to walk into the nearest town with my friends as they slowly but surely trickled out of the village and onto England. Each time I went to say good bye to someone, I kept trying to convince myself I'd be next, but no.

Nora Why?

Charlie Because of my Aunt.

Nora Your Aunt?

Charlie I couldn't leave her, I was her family. The only reason she had taken me in was because she had none of her own.

Nora She never married.

Charlie Oh, she did, but he was much older than her and it was more of a marriage of convenience,

Charlie	but when she never, shall we say fulfilled her part of the bargain, the convenience went out of it.
Nora	It must have been rough on her.
Charlie	It was, but then as she used to say, she had Charlie, her little boy Charlie. It just didn't matter how big her little boy got.
Nora	So you just stayed behind and watched all your friends leave.
Charlie	Yes.
Nora	That must have been hard on you.
Charlie	I got used to it.
Nora	Yes Charlie, like I got used to it, but that didn't mean, I didn't hate it.
Charlie	Good God, no Nora, I hated every minute of it, but it never finished. She had to know where I was all the time, just in case she needed help with something, and as she got older it got worse.
Nora	Charlie?

He stops and looks at her.

Nora	Well, I hope this doesn't sound silly, but if you never went away, or from the sounds of things met many people how do you know you are...
Charlie	Gay.

Nora tries to say it.

Charlie	It's ok, it's not catching you can say it.

Nora Gay.

Charlie I didn't really know when I was young, but what I did know was that I wasn't very interested in girls. At the time though I thought it might be because I was resentful towards my Aunt. So I tried, there was this girl that lived about a mile from us, her name was Mary, she was so pretty, little soft pink lips and long blonde hair. Everyone thought she was the prettiest girl around, I even have to admit I was mesmerised by her. So we courted for a while, all the lads were jealous and complained about how lucky I was. The funny thing was that I didn't feel as lucky as everyone thought I was. She wasn't much for talking and I wasn't much for necking. She got fed up with me after a while dumped me and never spoke to me again.

Nora But, that doesn't mean you're gay if you don't fancy one girl, maybe you should have seen others.

Charlie No Nora, it was after her I discovered. You see this boy, well he was sixteen at the time a year older than me, came to our village. He had been sent to stay with his cousins for the summer. I can remember the day I first saw him as clearly as if it was yesterday. I was driving the cattle home from the field, when there he was; sitting on one of the old stonewalls. He was sketching one of the trees in the field. I had never seen anyone so beautiful. His skin was so dark against his white shirt, the type we only ever wore to mass, and he had thick shiny black hair that fell cheekily in to his eyes. As I passed him, he looked up, nodded at me and my heart missed a beat. That was when I knew.

Nora You'd fallen in love.

Charlie Love at first sight.

Nora Did he feel the same way about you?

Charlie That was too much to wish for, or so I thought. I spent the entire summer trying to make up any excuse to pass the house he was staying in, but there was no sign of him, until one day when I had almost given up all hope, I saw him again in the same place we had first met. By this time I had given up hope and put all foolish ideas of anything happening out of my head. I was even embarrassed by my thoughts, which made me blush bright red as I approached him. But just as I got there he jumped off the wall and smiled at me. It was then I saw his eyes and knew he had to have felt the same way.

Nora So what happened?

Charlie He asked me to meet him as he was returning to England the following day. I told him it was difficult for me to get away, so he said he'd follow me back to my home and wait in the barn until all of my chores were done. That day everything seemed to take so long to do, but they had to be done well or my Aunt would be calling for me. Eventually, I got there; he was sitting in amongst the bails of straw, reading, when I arrived. He told me he had seen me all summer passing by his house but didn't have the courage to talk to me. He was afraid that he had imagined the feeling and that I could end up boxing him. As he spoke all I could do was look at his perfect lips as they moved around each word. He then became silent, we looked at each other and finally I raised the courage to touch him. I lifted my finger to his lips and then suddenly she started to call. 'Charlie, Charlie me boy, you know I need you Charlie'. He was so startled by her that he just ran away.

Nora Did you ever see him again?

Charlie No. And that's why I hate my name being said.

Nora Oh, I see.

Charlie There is one consolation though.

Nora Where?

Charlie As he ran away he forgot to take the book he was reading with him. When I found it, I felt like there was some hope. Then for the next

Charlie thirty years I sat in the barn every evening and read it over and over again.

Nora What was the book?

Charlie (Smiling) Romeo and Juliet by William Shakespeare.

Nora So that's why you like Shakespeare.

Charlie Yes, and I have a confession to make to you.

Nora Well?

Charlie I've never read any of his other plays; actually the only book I have ever read was that one.

Nora Now, I'm not so surprised about that, Charlie.

Charlie No?

Nora No. The thing I am most surprised about is how you stayed sane and had all this tied up in your heart.

Charlie For a while, I convinced myself that I would be able to go to England one day and find him. But as the years went by the dream just grew fainter. Then as my Aunt grew sicker I had

Charlie	more and more to do, so I tried not to think about it.
Nora	So when did you eventually leave the farm and move here?
Charlie	Five years ago.
Nora	Oh, Charlie.
Charlie	And I'm still looking after my Aunt.
Nora	You mean she's not dead.
Charlie	Goodness no, you can't kill a bad thing all that quickly. She had to have her leg amputated, gangrene had gotten into it, so she moved to an old folks' home. It's nearby; I go and visit her most days.
Nora	You know Charlie, I'm really sorry about earlier.
Charlie	It's ok.
Nora	I just didn't know how to react, and what's really silly is I reacted to you like I was afraid people would react to me if they found out I was illegitimate. I suppose we all have our own crosses to bear.
Charlie	It's just life Nora, that's all it is.
Nora	I don't know how you can feel all right about it all.
Charlie	I don't Nora, that's why I come here.
Nora	Your silent place.
Charlie	Precisely.

Nora I still don't quite understand though.

Charlie As I've said you will, you're almost there.

Nora Well, what do I have to do?

Charlie Just sit back and relax.

Nora sits back and she looks very relaxed. Charlie sits next to her. Silence. The sound of the city in the background slowly disappears.

Nora You know Charlie; this is the first time in years that I have felt this relaxed.

Charlie I felt that too when I found it.

Nora What?

Charlie The silent spaces between the memories.

Nora You're right, I'm not thinking about the past or what I have to do tomorrow, I'm just enjoying being here with you.

Charlie I'm glad.

Nora slides her hand over to touch Charlie's hand.

Nora Thank you.

She grabs his hand and squeezes it affectionately.

Charlie No, thank you Nora.

Nora What for?

Charlie Staying and listening.

Nora You know Charlie; I do feel like a lady here. I'm wthe lady over my entire life.

Charlie smiles.

Charlie		We never finished that dance, did we?

Nora		No.

Charlie stands up and gestures towards Nora.

Charlie		Well, my lady would you like to dance?

Nora		It would be a pleasure my lord.

They start to dance slowly. The music fades up.

Charlie		Friends?

Nora		Friends.

They start to laugh. Lights and music fades out slowly.

Further plays, books and writing by Tina O Rourke
is available on her website at www.tinaorourke.com.

Printed in Great Britain
by Amazon

57226046R00030

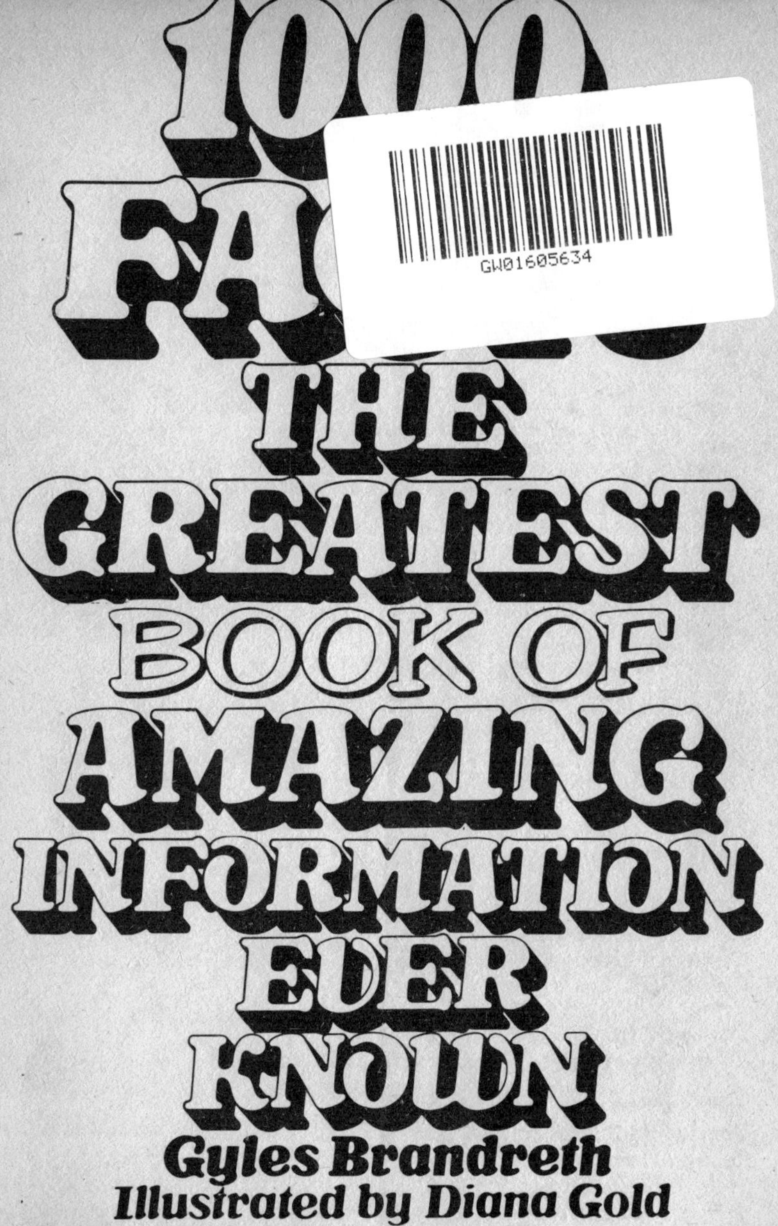

Gyles Brandreth
Illustrated by Diana Gold

CAROUSEL BOOKS
A DIVISION OF TRANSWORLD PUBLISHERS LTD

OTHER BOOKS BY GYLES BRANDRETH

THE DAFT DICTIONARY
THE BIG BOOK OF SECRETS
THE BIG BOOK OF PRACTICAL JOKES
THE BIG BOOK OF OPTICAL ILLUSIONS
JOKES JOKES JOKES A JOKE FOR EVERY DAY OF THE YEAR
1000 RIDDLES THE GREATEST BOOK OF RIDDLES EVER KNOWN
1000 QUESTIONS THE GREATEST QUIZ BOOK EVER KNOWN
1000 JOKES THE GREATEST BOOK OF JOKES EVER KNOWN
CHALLENGE
CRAZY DAYS
THE CRAZY BOOK OF WORLD RECORDS
THE BIG BOOK OF MAGIC
SHADOW SHOWS
THE CRAZY WORLD BOOK
THE CRAZY ENCYCLOPAEDIA

All published by CAROUSEL BOOKS

1000 FACTS THE GREATEST BOOK OF AMAZING INFORMATION EVER KNOWN
A CAROUSEL BOOK 0552 541656

First published in Great Britain 1980

PRINTING HISTORY
Carousel Edition published 1980
Carousel Edition reprinted 1981
Carousel Edition reprinted 1982

Carousel Books are published by
Transworld Publishers Ltd.
Century House,
61–63 Uxbridge Road,
Ealing, London W.5.

Phototypeset by Keyspools Ltd, Golborne, Lancs.
Made and printed in Great Britain by
The Guernsey Press Co. Ltd., Guernsey, Channel Islands.

You might find this **conversion table** useful:

The bold figures in the central columns can be read as either the metric or the British measure. So 1 inch = 25.4 millimetres, or 1 millimetre = 0.039 inches.

Inches		*Millimetres*	*Miles*		*Kilometres*
0.039	**1**	25.4	0.621	**1**	1.609
0.079	**2**	50.8	1.243	**2**	3.219
0.118	**3**	76.2	1.864	**3**	4.828
0.157	**4**	101.6	2.486	**4**	6.437
0.197	**5**	127.0	3.107	**5**	8.047
0.236	**6**	152.4	3.728	**6**	9.656
0.276	**7**	177.8	4.350	**7**	11.265
0.315	**8**	203.2	4.971	**8**	12.875
0.354	**9**	228.6	5.592	**9**	14.484

Feet		*Metres*	*Sq. Feet*		*Sq. Metres*
3.281	**1**	0.305	10.764	**1**	0.093
6.562	**2**	0.610	21.528	**2**	0.186
9.843	**3**	0.914	32.292	**3**	0.279
13.123	**4**	1.219	43.056	**4**	0.372
16.404	**5**	1.524	53.820	**5**	0.465
19.685	**6**	1.829	64.583	**6**	0.557
22.966	**7**	2.134	75.347	**7**	0.650
26.247	**8**	2.438	86.111	**8**	0.743
29.528	**9**	2.743	96.875	**9**	0.836

Cu. Feet		*Cu. Metres*	*Cu. Yards*		*Cu. Metres*
35.351	**1**	0.028	1.308	**1**	0.765
70.629	**2**	0.057	2.616	**2**	1.529
105.944	**3**	0.085	3.924	**3**	2.294
141.259	**4**	0.113	5.232	**4**	3.058
176.573	**5**	0.142	6.540	**5**	3.823
211.888	**6**	0.170	7.848	**6**	4.587
247.203	**7**	0.198	9.156	**7**	5.362
282.517	**8**	0.227	10.464	**8**	6.116
317.832	**9**	0.255	11.772	**9**	6.881

Pints		*Litres*	*Gallons*		*Litres*
1.760	**1**	0.568	0.220	**1**	4.546
3.520	**2**	1.137	0.440	**2**	9.092
5.279	**3**	1.705	0.660	**3**	13.638
7.039	**4**	2.273	0.880	**4**	18.184
8.799	**5**	2.841	1.100	**5**	22.731
10.559	**6**	3.410	1.320	**6**	27.277
12.318	**7**	3.978	1.540	**7**	31.823
14.078	**8**	4.546	1.760	**8**	36.369
15.838	**9**	5.114	1.980	**9**	40.915

Ounces		*Grams*	*Pounds*		*Kilograms*
0.036	**1**	28.350	2.205	**1**	0.454
0.071	**2**	56.699	4.409	**2**	0.907
0.106	**3**	85.049	6.614	**3**	1.361
0.141	**4**	113.398	8.819	**4**	1.814
0.176	**5**	141.748	11.023	**5**	2.268
0.212	**6**	170.097	13.228	**6**	2.722
0.247	**7**	198.447	15.432	**7**	3.175
0.282	**8**	226.796	17.637	**8**	3.629
0.317	**9**	255.146	19.842	**9**	4.082

Joseph Priestly (1733–1804) an English chemist, created soda water after watching the formation of gases during fermentation when he lived next door to a brewery.

Henry Burling (1801–1911) a first settler of Featherston, New Zealand lived to the age of 110 and at his death left 600 descendants.

A 54-year-old patient at Sedgefield General Hospital, was found to have swallowed 366 halfpennies, 26 sixpences, 17 threepences, 11 pennies, 4 shillings, and 27 pieces of wire.

An average human scalp has 100,000 hairs.

In Venezuela the young men partake in a sport called 'Toros coleados', which means pulling bulls by the tail.

There are at least 56 different groups of pure Indians now living in Mexico, each with its own language and culture.

There are 45 miles of nerves in the skin of a human being.

There is no soda in soda water.

The ‘tin can’ is 98 to $99\frac{1}{2}$ per cent steel.

Both sides of your face are never alike. The ears are not level, one eye is stronger than the other and the right ear is usually higher than the left.

It takes seventeen muscles to smile and forty-three muscles to frown.

A zebra’s stripes are as individual as human fingerprints.
No two zebras are striped alike.

A Japanese General had a moustache 20 inches long and on his death in 1933 it was buried with full honours in a separate casket.

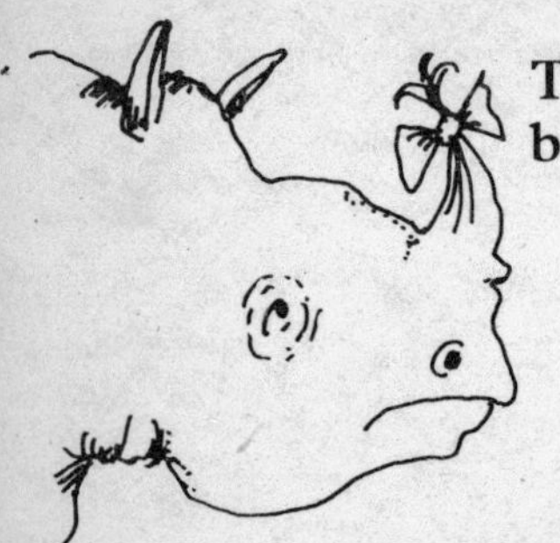

The horn of the rhinoceros is not bone, it is hair.

There are 22 miles more of canal in Birmingham than in Venice.

The books in the Bible attributed to Moses, David, Solomon and Daniel were all written long after they had died.

In the Japanese puppet theatre, the actors manipulate the puppets in full view of the audience.

There are about 60 permanent opera companies in West Germany.

A Canadian tattoo artist had 4,831 tattoos on his body.

In a chapel of the St Francis Monastery in Evora, Portugal, the walls and pillars are covered with human skulls and bones.

The platypus eats its own weight in worms every day.

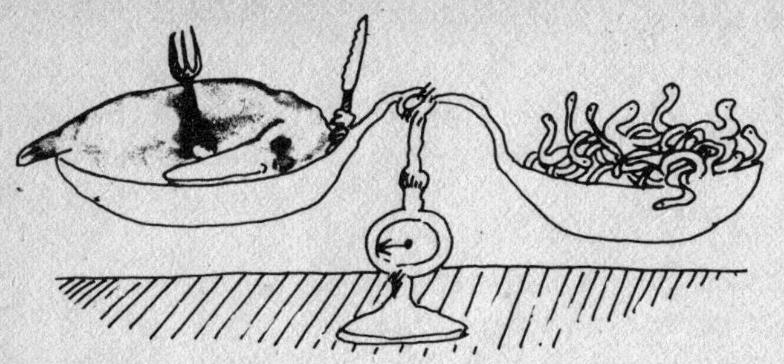

An ostrich egg is big enough to make a 12-man omelet.

Ostrich chicks grow about $1\frac{1}{2}$ metres in their first year.

Anthony Trollope, the novelist, was responsible for the postal pillarboxes in Britain.

The lead in the average pencil will draw a line 35 miles long.

Walking fast uses eight times as many calories as writing.

Mozart was playing and composing at the age of four.

A normal sized man weighs about forty times as much as his brain.

Oliver Cromwell was hanged and decapitated two years after his death.

At night a barn owl can see 100 times better than a human being.

Three hundred years ago King James I said 'Smoking is a custom loathsome to the eye, hateful to the nose, harmful to the brain, dangerous to the lungs.'

In Australia there were 100,000,000,000 rabbits before the introduction of myxomatosis in 1951.

It is impossible to sneeze and keep your eyes open at the same time.

The stump-tailed lizard of Australia has a tail that looks like its head.

A 17-year old girl of Miami, Florida, started to sneeze on 4th January 1966 and continued until 8th June 1966.

Over 70 per cent of the earth is covered by sea.

The largest-selling paperback ever published is *Baby and Child Care* by Dr Spock.

Forks only came into general use during the nineteenth century.

One day in 1945 so many starlings settled on the minute hand of Big Ben that it was slowed by 5 minutes.

To walk off 1 lb of fat, you would have to walk 34 miles.

One owl can eat 10 mice in a single meal which can save a farmer 360 lbs of vegetation a year.

When a car reaches the end of the assembly line, over 13,000 parts have been put together.

A fly moves its wings at the rate of 330 strokes a second.

King Richard I ruled for a period of ten years, but spent only about 6 months of his entire reign in England.

There are 28,000,000 cats in the USA.

The colour used for danger in scientific laboratories is not red, but bright yellow.

Queen Elizabeth I's courtiers regarded her as very fastidious because she took a bath once a month.

In Britain it is illegal to sell an animal as a pet to anyone under twelve.

Mayflies live for only a few hours.

The muscles required for an alligator to open its jaws are so weak a man can keep them closed with his hands.

The silkworm consumes 86,000 times its own weight in 56 days.

In 1972 a Swede balanced on one foot for $5\frac{1}{2}$ hours. Nothing could be used for balance or support.

Crocodiles have a semi-transparent third eyelid which slides over the eyes when they are submerged.

It is estimated that there are about 80 million people in the world with the surname Chang.

The floating island of Lake Alm in Upper Austria moves constantly from shore to shore.

The most widely cultivated fruit in the world is the apple. The second is the pear.

A single American oyster lays 500 million eggs a year – yet only one of them will normally reach maturity.

There are 206 bones in the human body.

A year-old Siamese cat in South Australia gave birth to 13 kittens.

The Rocking Stone, Cornwall, weighs several tons, yet can be rocked with a slight push.

A horseshoe was found in a tree in Salem, Oregon, US, embedded in the trunk. It had been there for 100 years, but was not rusty.

The muscles of the human jaw exert a force of over 219 kg.

The human mouth produces 2–3 pints of saliva a day.

In 1910 Dr Crippen was the first criminal to be arrested by the use of wireless communication.

The greater Dwarf Lemur of Madagascar always gives birth to triplets.

In 1962 an Adelaide (Australia) typist typed non-stop for 53 hours.

A statue of Marcus Aurelius astride a horse, in Rome, was used in the middle ages as a gallows – the rope was looped around the horse's head.

The nail on our middle finger-grows fastest. The nail on the thumb grows slowest.

An American skater, in 1965, jumped over 17 barrels.

Two-thirds of the body's weight is water.

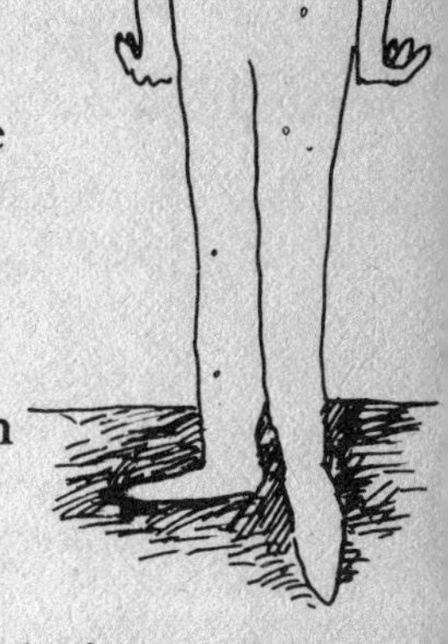

The red-capped Mangabey monkey of Africa communicates with its fellow monkeys by blinking its white eyelids, in a form of code.

Ninety-five per cent of the sun's matter consists of either hydrogen or helium.

The chance of quadruplets being born is about 1 for every 600,000 deliveries.

To make one tonne of paper, you need one tonne of coal.

Glen Miller's song 'Chattanooga Choo Choo' was the first to be awarded a golden disc for selling over one million copies.

The most common disease in the world is tooth decay.

George Washington used to soak his ivory dentures every night in port to improve their flavour.

A ten-year-old Californian boy sat in a tree in his backyard for 55 days.

In London in the middle of the eighteenth century, nearly 75 per cent of the babies born died before the age of five.

Tea was first imported into Europe by the Dutch East India Company in 1609.

A pickpocket deported to Australia for his crimes, there became chief of police of Parramatta.

In the middle of the nineteenth century one and a half million Irish died during the Potato Famine.

William Shakespeare spelt his surname eleven different ways.

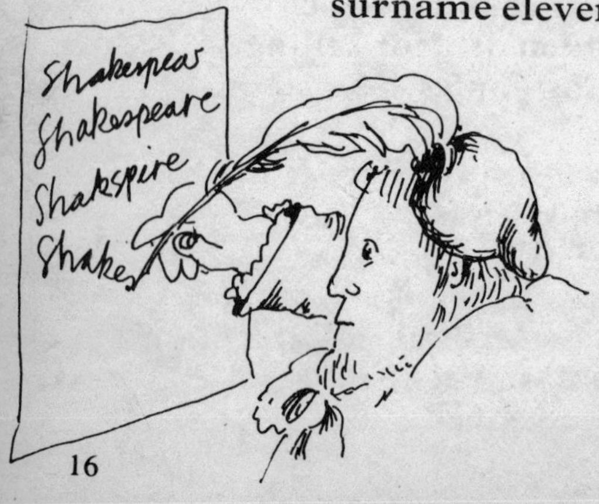

Damascus is the oldest inhabited capital city in the world.

An ounce of gold can be beaten into a sheet covering 9.3 square metres, or drawn into 80.5 km (50 miles) of wire.

John Bunyan wrote most of *A Pilgrim's Progress* whilst serving a six-month prison sentence in Bedford Jail.

An anagram of 'funeral' is 'real fun'.

Between 1930 and 1934 there were no speed limits on British roads.

The honeycomb made by bees is hexagonal in shape because that allows the maximum space using the least amount of wax.

The highest motor road in Europe is that leading to the peak of Picacho de Veleta, Spain. It reaches an altitude of 11,450 feet.

There is a set of traffic lights in Venice which controls the junction of two canals.

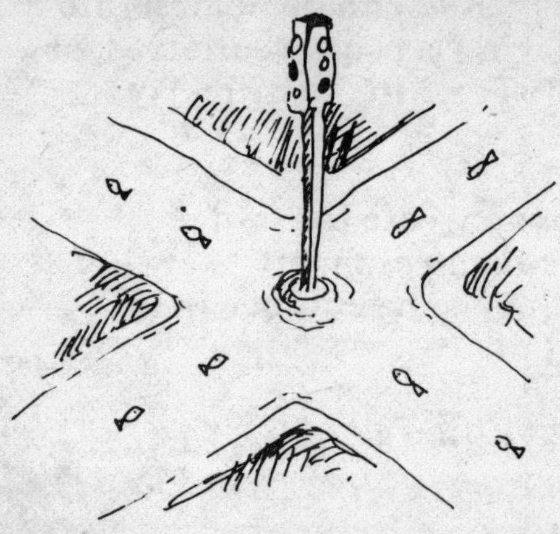

A bottle of wine sold in London in 1960 was 420 years old.

If you travelled south from Vancouver Island on the west coast of Canada, you would not touch land until you reached Antarctica.

In theory the lowest possible temperature is −273.15°C, absolute zero.

A column of pennies 3 metres high was collected in London for charity.

The United States Library of Congress contains 73 million volumes, housed on 350 miles of shelving.

Leonardo da Vinci could write with one hand and draw with the other at the same time.

In 1888 in Moradabad, Northern India, 246 people were killed by hailstones.

The giant squid, whose length can exceed 15 metres, has the largest eyes of any living animal; they measure 38 cms across.

Between 1851 and 1852 55 boys under fourteen were sent to prison for stealing less than sixpence.

In the 1920s a census taken among Eskimos showed that less than one in forty-six had ever seen an igloo.

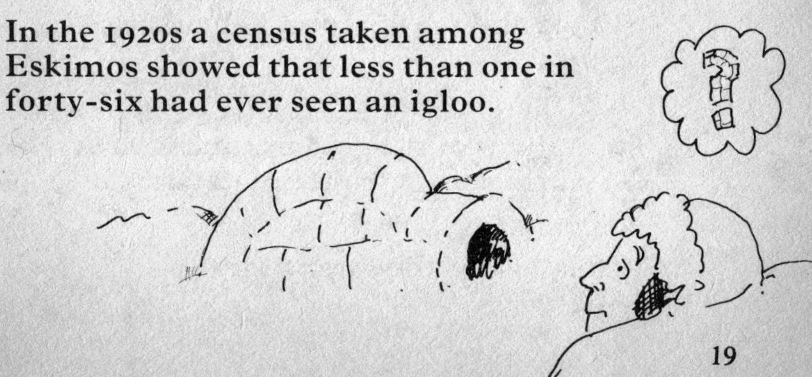

A 14-year old French girl had extraordinary electrical powers. With a gentle touch she could knock over heavy pieces of furniture and people in physical contact with her received an electric shock.

Flogging was only abolished in the British Army and Navy in 1881.

A mother in Sydney, Australia, gave birth to twins 56 days apart and in different years; one born December 16, 1952 and the other on February 10, 1953.

Two-thirds of the gold produced in the world comes from South Africa.

Minus 40°C is the same as minus 40°F.

The bathtub used by President William Taft, in the White House, USA, was so huge to hold his great bulk, that four workmen once sat in it comfortably.

The Apache Indian Geronimo, who terrorised the southwest of America during the 1880s, ended his days selling his photograph for 25 cents each.

Peers never wear gloves in the House of Lords when the sovereign is present.

Of all the world's major languages, English has the largest vocabulary – about 800,000 words.

A street in Guanajuat, Mexico, is so narrow that sweethearts can kiss each other across their opposite balconies.

By 1776 George IV as Prince of Wales, had amassed debts which would be equal to £12 million today.

In Queanbeyan, Australia, there is a tandem which carries 31 people.

British gold sovereigns and half sovereigns were replaced by treasury notes in 1914.

Tattooing on the chin was once a sign of high rank among the Maoris of New Zealand, and though no longer practised, it is quite common among the elders.

Fans were found in the tomb of Tutankahman, with their ostrich feathers intact after more than 3,000 years.

Rossini, the Italian composer, wrote 38 operas in the first 37 years of his life, and though he lived for another 39 years, never wrote another one.

The giraffe is about 1.2 m. taller than a double-decker bus.
In spite of its long neck it has poor vocal cords and has only 7 bones in its neck, the same as man.

A frog's tongue grows from the front of its mouth, which allows for a longer reach when catching insects.

In 1905 a man ran up the 729 steps of the Eiffel Tower in Paris in 3 minutes 12 seconds.

One-sixth of the land area of the earth is to be found within the boundaries of the USSR.

At least one person in ten in Great Britain plays darts.

After Sir Walter Raleigh was executed in 1618, his widow had his head embalmed and carried it in a red leather bag wherever she went until her own death twenty-nine years later.

Israel is the only country in the world which has compulsory military service for women.

Only the mother can be charged with infanticide. Any other parties may be charged with murder.

In 1972 a black and white cat fell 49 metres from a building in Toronto and survived.

A camera marketed in France in 1882 was shaped like a pistol.

In 1925–27 a Swiss schoolmaster rode horseback from Buenos Aires, Argentina, to Washington, D.C. – a distance of 10,000 miles.

The tip of a kiwi's beak is so sensitive it can detect worms deep in the ground.

The cave swifts of Southeast Asia build nests out of saliva. The Chinese use these nests to make birds nest soup.

Alcohol cannot be absorbed into the bloodstream in quantities strong enough to kill germs.

A single drop of water contains one hundred billion billion atoms.

The oldest recorded age at which someone has had a surgical operation is 111 years 105 days. Born July 25, 1849, died February 10, 1961, Henry Brett of Houston, Texas, underwent an operation on November 7, 1960.

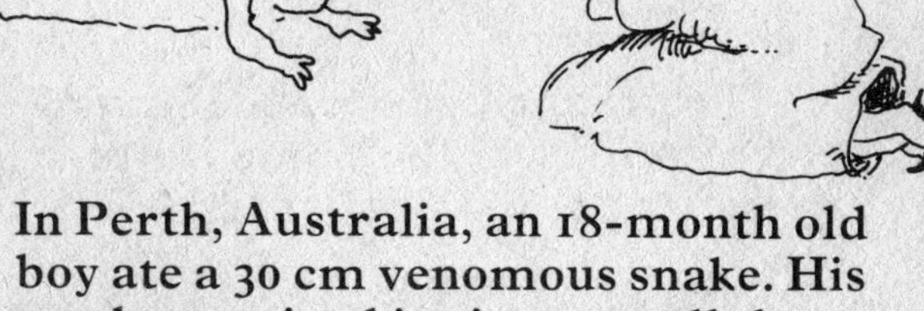

In Perth, Australia, an 18-month old boy ate a 30 cm venomous snake. His mother arrived in time to pull the tail end from his mouth – he was unharmed.

There are more acres in Yorkshire than words in the Bible.

The longest vehicular tunnel in the world is the London Underground line from Morden to East Finchley; it is 17 miles 528 yards long.

The first all-British motor car was the 1895 Lanchester.

One in ten of the men who died in Britain in 1976 died of lung cancer.

The first Olympics were held in Athens in 1896, with nine nations competing.

The first bridge over the River Tiber in Rome, was the Ponte Rotto, which was in use for 1,717 years.

The tuatara lizard of New Zealand is a living fossil. It is the only survivor of an order of reptiles common 250 million years ago. It takes at least a year for its eggs to incubate.

The oldest English bank was founded in 1603 by Francis Child.

A message in a bottle dropped by an American ship in 1941 floated 1250 miles across the Pacific in 53 days, but the native who found it could not understand any of the eight languages in which it was written.

Candles are sometimes set up around the coffin of a dead person. This is a relic of an old superstition that evil spirits would enter the corpse and fires were lit around it to keep them out.

The oldest international cricket match was played between the USA and Canada in 1844.

In April 1884 there was an earthquake which killed four people in East Anglia.

There is a natural sauna on a beach in Japan created by steam from an underground volcano, and men and women cover themselves with the sand.

The humming bird can fly backwards, sideways, forwards, and hover motionless for up to an hour.

The permanent wave, which made millions for hair-dressers, was invented by Charles Nessler, yet when he died in 1951 only one hair-dresser attended his funeral.

Yehudi Menuhin gave his first public concert when he was eight years old.

Two and a half times more beer than wine is drunk in Luxembourg.

In Spitzbergen, Norway at one time of the year the sun shines continuously for three and a half months.

In 1975 a company based in Cambridge exported 1800 tonnes of sand to the desert state of Abu Dhabi in the Persian Gulf.

The Danish flag, a white cross on a red ground, is the oldest national flag, and was introduced in 1219.

Deer grow new antlers each year – antelope do not.

In order to be the last name in the local telephone directory, a Chicago man changed his name to Zeke Zzzypt.

The Spring Peeper is the smallest of all frogs, measuring only one inch.

The volume of water in the Amazon is greater than the combined total volume of the next eight largest rivers in the world.

The elephant has 40,000 muscles in its trunk but not a single bone.

The chances of a mother giving birth to quadruplets are about 1 in 600,000.

In Saudi Arabia there is an area of 250,000 square miles, known as 'The Empty Quarter' where practically no life of any kind exists.

The average person consumes about one tonne of food and drink every year.

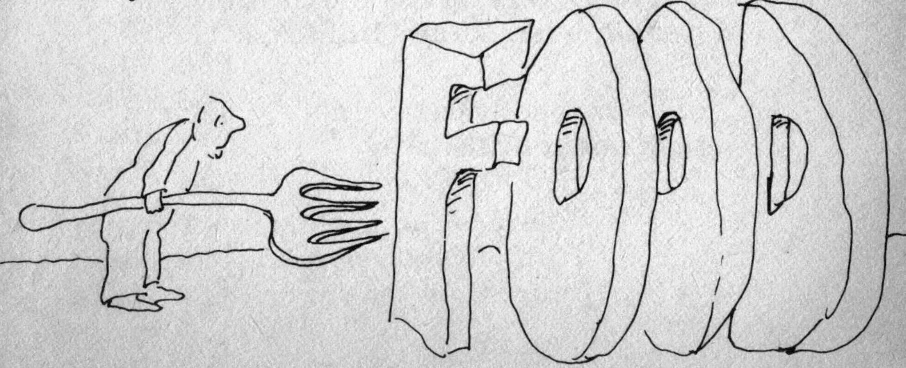

In colonial America shoes could be worn on either foot.

Both North and South America could be fitted into Asia with room to spare.

For many years ravens were stealing golf balls from a course in Lithgow, Australia, So ping-pong balls filled with pepper, mustard and milk have caused them to cease the habit.

The eighteenth-century name for a butcher was a 'flesh-flogger'.

Despite its large size and fierce looks, the gorilla is a peaceable animal. It is a vegetarian and lives in a nest made of sticks and branches.

The dragonfly can see a flying gnat at a distance of 18 feet.

There is enough hard coal in the Ruhr, West Germany, to last for more than 400 years.

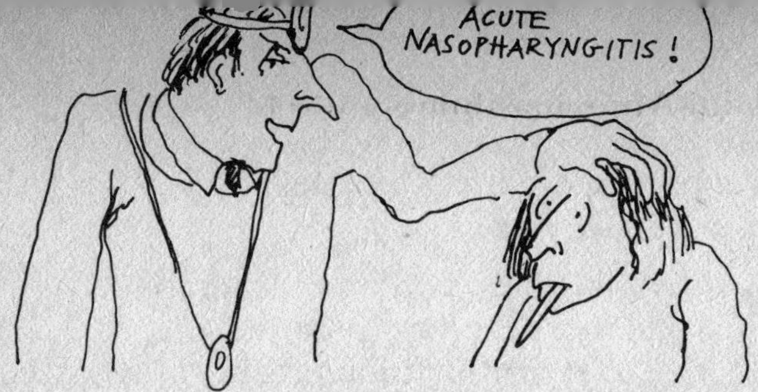

The scientific name for the common cold is 'acute nasopharyngitis'.

A woman of the Toda tribe of southern India gets only two garments in her lifetime, one in childhood and the second when she is married.

Frozen ducks crashed out of the sky in Arkansas, USA, for ten minutes one morning in 1974. They had flown into a belt of cold air and froze to death.

America is named after Amerigo Vespucci, an Italian explorer who was the first to discover the American mainland in 1499.

During the seven years he was Poet Laureate Wordsworth did not in fact write any poetry.

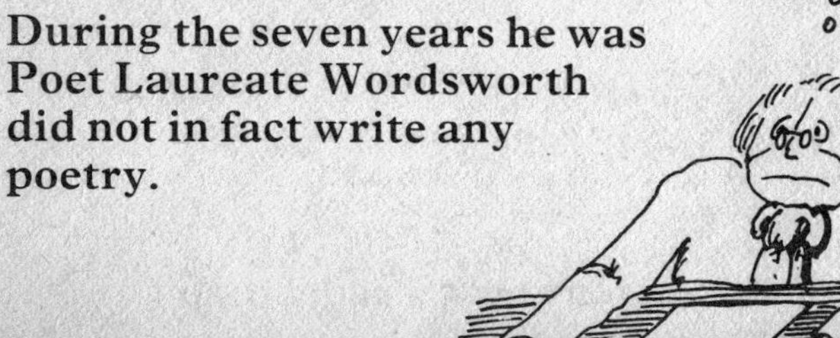

A French scientist discovered how to make paper from wood by watching wasps make paper-like nests by chewing up food.

An Indian poem called the 'Mahabharata' contains almost three million words.

There is nearly three times as much energy in 100 g of butter as in 100 g of steak.

During the Black Death in the middle of the fourteenth century 75 million people died.

When giraffes are shipped to zoos the greatest problem to face is not their necks, but their legs, which break very easily. If a giraffe slips, chances are his legs will double under him and snap.

A Melbourne man once skipped 286 times in one minute, averaging almost five turns a second.

In 1936 Jesse Owens beat a racehorse over a 100 yards sprint.

In 1888 the cotton crop of America was being destroyed by an insect pest, so thousands of Australian ladybirds were imported and within 2 years had brought the pest under control.

King Charles I was only 4 ft. 7 ins tall.

George Washington, the first President of the United States, was a champion wrestler and long-jumper.

Natives of the Puamo Islands in the Eastern Pacific wear a dancing garment made from the hair of their departed ancestors.

A lieutenant in the Soviet airforce fell 6,700 metres without a parachute; he landed in a snow-covered ravine.

The first roadside petrol pump in Britain was installed in Newbury, Berkshire, in 1920.

The British spend twice as much on pet food as on baby food.

The card game, Bridge, originated in Turkey.

A citizen of Cedar Rapids' Iowa, swam 25 yards on his back balancing a ladder on his chin.

There is a bye-law in New York which forbids women from smoking in the street and public places.

Chief Sitting Bull, credited with wiping out General Custer's forces, was actually a medicine man and stayed behind the lines at Little Big Horn.

A Hindu fakir, in the USA, lay on a bed of needle-sharp nails for 25 hours 20 minutes.

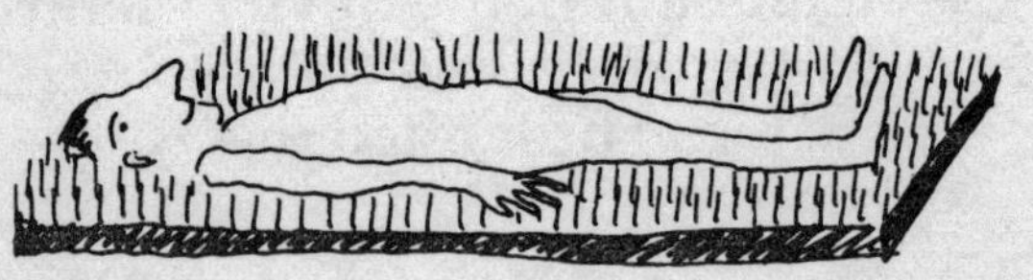

The highest falls are the Angel Falls in Venezuela, at over 900 metres high.

A popular dish in Wales is Bara lawd, made from washed seaweed mixed with oatmeal and bacon.

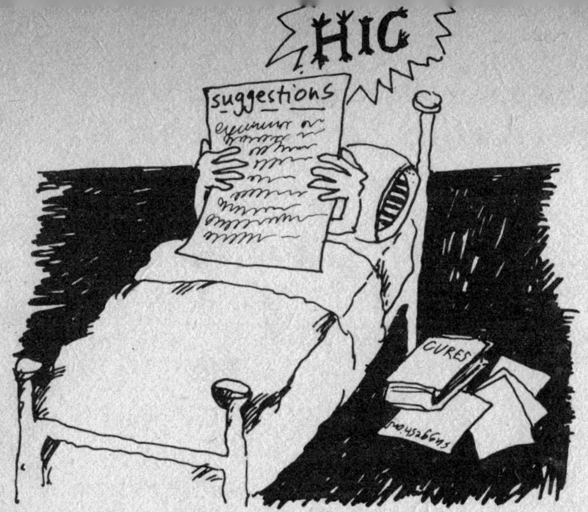

From 13th June 1948 to 1st June 1958 a citizen of Los Angeles hiccoughed 160,000,000 times. People sent 60,000 suggestions for cures.

The first traffic signals installed outside the Houses of Parliament in 1868 blew up and killed a policemen – the signals had red and green gas lamps.

By the end of the seventeenth century half the population of England never ate meat.

Between 1603 and 1665 there had only been four plague-free years in London.

Ice-cream was invented by a Frenchman called Gerald Tissain in 1620.

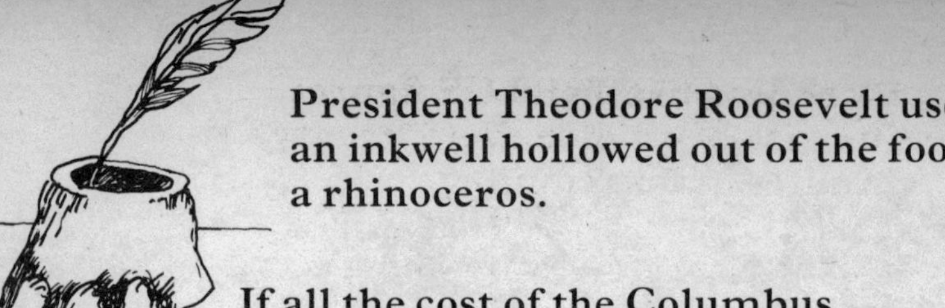

President Theodore Roosevelt used an inkwell hollowed out of the foot of a rhinoceros.

If all the cost of the Columbus expedition that led to the discovery of America were added up it would amount to little over £3,500 in terms of today's money.

Baked beans were originally served with molasses; tomato sauce was substituted in 1880, fifty years after their introduction.

The small Greek island of Mikonos has 365 churches built on it.

Even in 1539 during the reign of Henry VIII it was still possible for a man to be hanged in London for eating meat on a Friday.

The 'golden disc' awarded to singers whose sales top a million contains 0·03 grammes of gold – worth sixpence in 1969.

A tombstone of a teacher in Elkhart, Indiana, USA, reads 'School is out, Teacher has gone home.'

According to official US figures there is one suicide every twenty minutes in that country.

In 1871 George Westinghouse, engineer and manufacturer, introduced Saturday afternoons off for his workers, and holidays with pay.

A citizen of West Australia carried a 38 kg brick in a downward position in an ungloved hand, a distance of 64 km.

All of Queen Anne's seventeen children died before their mother.

There is no place in England that is more than 75 miles from the sea.

Drops of water thrown onto a red-hot surface never actually touch the surface but rest on a cushion of vapour until they evaporate.

Fortune tellers are still liable to punishment under the 1824 Vagrancy Act.

The male midwife toad carries the eggs laid by its mate like a bunch of grapes attached to its back.

The most efficient form of light production so far discovered is the glow-worm.

There are 444 mosques in Istanbul.

An English boy ate 1,220 cold beans, one at a time with a cocktail stick, in 30 minutes.

The emperor penguin shields its young from the cold by hobbling along with the chick between its feet.

More than 95 per cent of the fish caught in the world are caught in the northern hemisphere.

About one million meteors reach our atmosphere every hour.

The Lucanus Cervus beetle lives only a few weeks, yet its larva lives 4 years.

The practice of baptising children with a double Christian name was unknown in England until the time of the Stuarts.

The Blister Bush found in South Africa, when touched causes large painful blisters.

New-born ducks do not appear to know how to swim.

Draftsmen have to make 27,000 drawings for the manufacture of a new car.

Shirley Temple made over $1,000,000 before she was ten.

Richard III, Louis XIV and Napoleon Bonaparte were all born with teeth.

In 1885 a 24-year old girl jumped 76 metres from Clifton Suspension Bridge and landed unhurt. Her voluminous dress and petticoats acted as a parachute.

Bats catch insects and avoid objects in their path by emitting squeaks, then listening for the echoes to return.

During a bullfight in Malaga, Spain, the matador rested an arm on the forehead of the bull and held the beast's horn in his mouth.

Four babies are born every second.

The wheeled transport vehicle is 1,000 years older than the road.

Queen Anne was the first to suggest racing horses at Ascot.

Horseshoes came into use about 100 B.C.

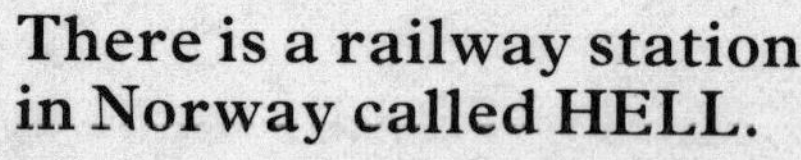

There is a railway station in Norway called HELL.

Aspirin occurs naturally in the bark of certain trees.

DDT had been known for sixty years before it was first used.

The Aborigines of Australia used moulds from the shady side of trees to treat wounds centuries before Alexander Fleming discovered penicillin.

The safety pin was invented in the Mediterranean region during the Bronze Age.

King Edward VIII is the only British sovereign to write an autobiography.

The 1933 King Kong was a hand puppet 6 ins high.

King James I wrote a book against smoking, in 1604. It was entitled 'Counterblast against Tobacco.'

The deepest crater made by a meteorite is in Arizona and is 1,200 metres wide.

The patron saint of Ireland, Saint Patrick, was not an Irishman but was born on the west coast of Britain.

An Alsatian's sense of smell is a million times better than a man's.

A spirit house is erected at dangerous corners in Thailand, to placate the evil spirits that cause traffic accidents.

It is estimated that there are 200 million left-handed people in the world.

Early Christians did not use altars, which originated in pagan worship, and were introduced into churches later.

The largest cabbage recorded was grown in 1865 by a citizen of Co. Durham, which grew to a circumference of 259 inches, and weighed 123 lbs.

A 12-year-old English boy completed 11,052 jumps on his pogo stick in 1971.

A thunderstorm in Lapleau in France in 1968 occurred during which lightning struck a flock of sheep, killing all the black ones, but leaving the white ones untouched.

Durham Cathedral was started in 1093 and work was still being done on it in 1500.

A curious plant, the rafflesia, grows in Indonesia. It grows on shrubs and vines, sending fibrous roots into them. Then when it produces its single flower, all the other external parts have withered away and only the flower is visible.

The religious practice of kissing the Pope's toe lasted for over 1000 years before being abolished in 1773.

The last European witch was burned in Switzerland in 1782.

The Earl of Stirling rented the whole of Canada from King James I of Scotland for one penny a year.

Between the ages of 1 and 14 in the United States more people die from accidents than from disease.

The patients of African witch – doctors are upset if they don't get a bill. If the patient is going to die, there is no fee.

Marie de Medici, Queen of France, owned a dress which at today's prices would cost £5 million. She wore it only once.

The exclamation point (!) comes from the Greek word 'lo' meaning 'I am surprised'.

In 1970 a Texan swallowed 225 live goldfish.

In terms of sales of single records, the most successful song-writer is Paul McCartney, former Beatle.

One of the wettest places on earth is in Hawaii, where the rainfull averages 471.68 inches,

More tea is drunk in the Republic of Ireland per person than in any other country.

Bricks are the oldest construction materials manufactured by man and were used in Egypt 7000 years ago.

Einstein did not believe in the use of shaving soap, and only shaved with warm water.

The plot for 'Dr Jekyll and Mr Hyde' came to Robert Louis Stevenson in a nightmare.

The female angler fish carries her tiny 'husband' attached to her underside.

An elephant can carry 2 gallons of water in its trunk.

Thirty thousand people died in an earthquake which hit the city of St Pierre on the Caribbean island of Martinique in 1908. The only survivor was a prisoner in the city's gaol.

There are 3,000 sweat glands to every square inch of skin in the palms of our hands.

Benito Mussolini, dictator of Italy, was twice expelled from school for assaulting fellow students with a knife.

A Rhodesian was stung by 2,443 bees, and lived.

The desert lynx catches birds by leaping into the air.

The Battle of Hastings was fought at Senlac Hill, 6 miles from Hastings.

One prong of the antlers of male reindeer protects an eye from injury in their furious battles with other males.

Running flat out a hare can reach 45 mph.

Australian aborigines who are widowers wear blobs of mud in their beard to show they are seeking another wife.

The starfish has an eye on the end of each arm.

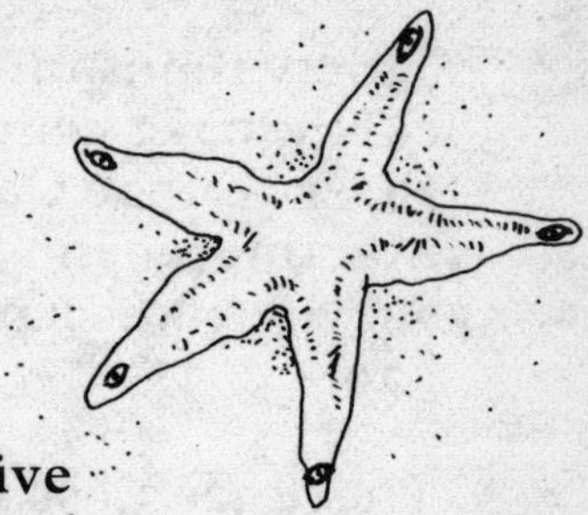

Eight hundred and forty-five different dialects are spoken in India.

A society campaigning against alcoholism in northern Australia had to disband because of lack of support.

George Gershwin, famous American composer, was a professional pianist at the age of 15.

Cat gut comes from sheep.

The candle fish of the American Pacific is so oily that the Indians tie them to sticks to make torches.

Our nerves transmit messages at up to 300 ft per second.

There are eight cities called Rome in the USA.

The long-tailed sheep of India pull a small 2-wheeled cart which supports their 10lb tail.

The Badshahi Mosque in Lahore, Pakistan, is the largest mosque in the world, and can accommodate 100,000 in the courtyard where services are held. It was built in 1671.

The screwdriver was invented before the screw. It was originally used to extract bent nails.

Fred Astaire's legs were insured for $650,000.

On New Year's Day 1907 president Theodore Roosevelt of the USA shook hands with 513 people.

In Lorentz Weiler, Luxembourg, there is a church, St Mary's, located in a mountain cave.

The last prisoner to be held in the Tower of London was the Nazi, Rudolf Hess, who was imprisoned there during the Second World War.

Baby seals are born on land and have to be taught how to swim by their parents.

George IV was created Earl of Chester when he was seven days old.

On the Jungfrau mountain in Switzerland there is a hall of ice containing piano, stove and tables, carved out of solid ice.

Only the cock nightingale sings.

During the fourteen years of prohibition in the United States over 7000 people were killed in gang fights.

A chair made for King John VI of Portugal incorporated a hearing aid, in the form of lions' mouths in the chair's arms. People used to speak through the mouths which acted as acoustics.

A fully grown human brain weights about 3 lbs.

Guinea pigs were domesticated by Incas 2,000 years ago and are still used by the Indians of South America for food.

The first ship to sail round the world was the *Victoria*, commanded by Ferdinand Magellan, in 1519–22.

We blink twenty-five times each minute.

The lop-eared sheep of North Africa has a coat that is half wool and half hair.

The Canadian capital, Ottawa, has an anti-noise law which prohibits the buzzing of bees.

A chameleon's tongue is often twice as long as its body.

The tarantula is one of the few spiders unable to spin a web.

A man and woman in Mexico City were engaged for 67 years and finally married at the age of 82.

The giant squid is the largest living animal without a backbone.

A flea can jump over 200 times its own length.

A codfish weighs 5000 times as much as its brain.

In October 1961 a new volcano on the island of Tristan da Cunha in the Atlantic rose to a height of 90 feet in a few hours.

The albatross has a hooked beak with which it can exert as much force as a pickaxe.

The word 'police' did not appear in official English until 1714. It was originally a French word.

In 1970 29 students of the City of London College, piled on top of an oval pillar box.

Wordsworth and Tennyson both borrowed the same suit from their fellow poet, Samuel Rogers, when they went to Buckingham Palace to be invested as Poet Laureate.

If all the blood vessels in the human body were laid end to end they would stretch 100,000 miles.

The Prince of Wales, later King Edward VII, was the first member of the Royal Family to own and drive a motor car.

Male crickets 'sing' by rubbing their wings together. Their chirps vary according to the temperature.

A kangaroo cannot jump with its tail off the ground.

The paddlefish found in the Mississippi river catches food merely by swimming along with its mouth open.

There are 7 miles of lift shafts in the Empire State Building, New York.

There is an average of one suicide a month from the Golden Gate Bridge in San Francisco.

George Sand, the French woman novelist, never wrote in the daytime, doing all her writing between the hours of 10 pm and 5 am.

The badger is the largest land carnivore living in the British Isles.

More British troops were killed at the one-day battle of Malplaquet in 1709 than in the ten-day battle of El Alamein.

Both Alexander the Great and Julius Caesar were epileptics.

Dormice were a popular delicacy in Ancient Rome.

The Great Blue Heron catches fish by spearing them with its bill.

The wrinkled grey covering of the brain is made up of 9,000,000,000 cells.

There are six languages in north America which each have only one surviving speaker.

Ladies in sixteenth and seventeenth century England wore their wedding ring on their thumb.

A superintendent of nurses in the American Civil War refused to employ any nurse who was pretty.

On average we lose 11 oz of weight while we are asleep at night.

A girl in Perth, Australia, can read at 100,000 words per minute. In half an hour she read Hamlet, Wuthering Heights, and several short stories.

The official languages of the United Nations are Chinese, English, French, Russian and Spanish.

The Romans used weasels to catch mice.

If all the corks of all the wine bottles produced in France each year were glued together, they would encircle the earth ten times.

Andrew Jackson at the age of 78 became the first US President to have his picture taken.

Ivan the Terrible killed his favourite son in a burst of anger.

$7\frac{1}{2}$ million tonnes of water evaporate from the Dead Sea every day.

Four boys of the Central Grammar School, Birmingham, played darts continuously for 150 hours in 1972.

The human body contains enough phosphorus to make the heads of 2000 matches, enough fat for seven bars of soap and enough iron to make one nail.

A 16-year old American did 6,006 press-ups in 3 hrs 54 minutes in 1965.

The first despatch from the Duke of Marlborough announcing his victory at Blenheim was written on the back of a tavern bill.

Originally the yo-yo was a Filipino jungle weapon.

A pride of 22 lions killed 1500 Kenyans in one year.

Charles Frohman (1860–1915) was a Broadway producer, who owned a theatre, and controlled 5 others, managed 28 stars, and at his death left a net estate of $451.

A horse has eighteen pairs of ribs, a human being has twelve.

Ambulances were developed by Napoleon's surgeon in his Italian campaign of 1796–7.

King Alexander of Greece was bitten by a pet monkey in 1920 and died of blood poisoning.

Cars were first started by ignition in 1949.

Statuettes found in tombs in Changsha, China, revealed that the Chinese invented stirrups 1,675 years ago.

Crushed strawberries are useful for cleaning teeth and for relieving sunburn.

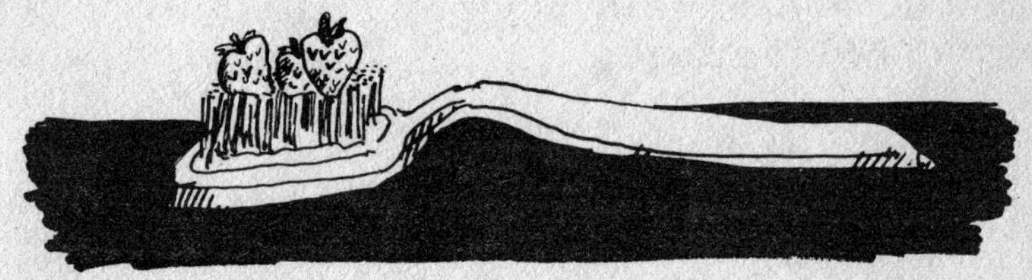

A snail can crawl over a razor-blade without cutting itself.

During their studies medical students increase their vocabulary by 10,000 words.

Almost one-eighth of the world's surface receives less than 25 cms (9.8 ins) of rain a year.

An oak tree in Florida, USA, has a palm tree growing from it.

In 1348 88 cases of murder were recorded in Yorkshire.
A modern equivalent would be around 10,000 a year.

Two American students played table tennis continuously for 36 hours.

A monument at Le Cailar, France, marks the grave of a bull who was noted for its bravery in the bullring.

The complete skin covering of the body measures about 20 square feet.

Teddy Bears were named after the American President, Theodore Roosevelt.

Charles II was nicknamed 'Old Rowley' after his favourite horse.

The cheetah is the fastest animal over a short distance. Up to 600 metres it can run at 113 kph.

The Japanese railway system is the busiest in the world and professional 'pushers' are employed to push in passengers before the doors can be closed.

Frederick the Great of Prussia used to drink coffee made with champagne.

Today half the total dead in Britain are cremated.

The coffins in which chiefs of the Wangata tribe of the Congo are buried, are carved in the shapes of men and women.

In 1973 a freak storm of thousands of small frogs hit the village of Brignoles in southern France.

A Stoke Newington dentist pulled out a tooth from a woman patient, and a centipede crawled out of it.

In the Solomon Islands lengths of vegetable fibre plaited with flying fox teeth were used as money.

A citizen of Spanish Fork, Utah, has lived in the house in which he was born, for 90 years.

Marbles were introduced into Britain by the Romans in the first century A.D.

Approximately 21,500 species of insects are found in England.

Cannon-balls were used in the Royal Navy until they were replaced by shells in 1837.

The female cicada can hear her mate calling a mile away.

Humming birds can beat their wings 90 times a second.

Insects are eaten as food in many parts of the world, the favourites being grasshoppers, beetles, crickets, locusts, termites, and ants.

The oil in which sardines are packed is more expensive by volume than the fish themselves.

The earliest blood transfusions used animals' blood.

The stegosaurus weighed $6\frac{1}{2}$ tonnes, but its brain weighed only 71 grammes.

The only member of the British Royal Family to have competed at the Wimbledon tennis championships was King George VI.

In Florida, USA, the rattlesnake is served as an hors d'oeuvres.

Enid Blyton wrote a total of 600 children's stories.

Cockroaches are commonly called 'black beetles', but they are not black and it is not a beetle.

Jean-Paul Sartre, French novelist, taught himself to read and write.

An English firm made a jigsaw puzzle for an American consisting of 10,400 pieces, and measuring 4.6 metres × 3 metres.

Beetles outnumber any other living creatures on earth.

There are 3700 species found in Britain alone.

In the Second World War 22.2 per cent of the population of Poland was killed.

In the Northern Punjab in India, a woman isn't considered to be correctly dressed unless she wears nose rings.

The manufacturers of 'Monopoly' print more 'money' than the whole of the United States Treasury.

Children of the Nanay tribe in Siberia live long distances from school and travel there by skis pulled by dogs.

Saudi Arabia covers an area of 830,000 square miles, yet there is not a single river in the whole country.

It is illegal to sell anti-freeze to Indians in Quebec, Canada.

In 1965 a Japanese created a slow-bicycling record by remaining stationary for 5 hours 25 minutes.

Hundreds of fossil jellyfish found in Australia, prove that the area was covered by the sea 600 million years ago.

A temple to the 'God of Food' in Nepal, is decorated with countless offerings of pots and pans.

Blackberries are used to make wine, hair-dye, cough medicine, and a refreshing drink.

Roman senators used to wear purple stripes in their togas as a mark of their rank.

Buckingham Palace contains 602 rooms.

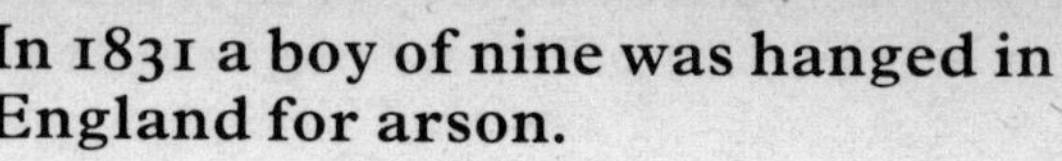

In 1831 a boy of nine was hanged in England for arson.

A Hungarian wrote 32 lines of words on a single match stick.

The mother of US President Ulysses S. Grant was often in Washington during her son's presidency, but never visited him at the White House.

A citizen of Calcutta, India, grew the fingernails on his left hand to a length of 76 inches.

A crowd estimated at between 60,000 and 70,000 attended the funeral in October 1973 of marathon champion Abebe Bikila of Ethiopia.

The smallest independent country in the world is Vatican City – with a zero birth rate.

A Yorkshire woman succeeded in gaining her driving licence at her fortieth attempt.

The first occasion when a flag was flown at half-mast as a mark of respect for the dead was in 1612. It was lowered to half-mast when the captain of a ship had been killed by Eskimos.

Man-made satellites were first suggested by Sir Isaac Newton in a work published in 1687.

In India in 1970 there was a school in the Jamma district with one pupil and one teacher.

A hippopotamus can run faster than a man.

Louis Braille who invented a system of reading for the blind, developed it from messages used by French troops who punched marks in paper so they could be read at night without the use of light.

When the Palace of Versailles was built there were no bath-rooms or lavatories in the whole of the building.

The last British king to take part in a battle was George II at the Battle of Dettingen in 1743.

Anna Karenina, heroine of Leo Tolstoy's book, died in a railway station. In 1910 Tolstoy himself died in a railway station.

State Treasurer of Texas in the 1930s was a 3-foot 9-inch midget.

In Killarney, Ireland, at the Eagle's Nest Cave, you will be told that if you sound a bugle note there you will hear it repeated at least a hundred times.

The Portuguese Man-o'-War (jelly-fish) is not one single animal but a colony of small animals.

Between 1500 and 1600 the stock of precious metals in Europe trebled.

The diprotodon (or giant wombat) lived in Australia 500,000 years ago in large numbers. It was the same size as a rhinoceros.

In Norway many cottages have grass roofs.

There are known to be 1000 million galaxies in the universe – there may be many more.

Attila the Hun was a dwarf.

There have been only thirteen convictions made from over 1000 Chicago murders committed in the last sixty years.

A citizen of Michigan USA received a postcard in February 1976 that had been mailed 68 years before addressed to his grandfather.

In most countries more women than men attempt suicide, but more men succeed in their attempts.

In Queensland, Australia, there is a wild-goat milking contest – but competitors have first to catch their goat.

Queen Elizabeth I had 2,000 gowns which were kept in a separate clothing house.

A Chicago man at the age of 63 walked a mile an hour for 1,000 consecutive hours.

Jack the Ripper was left-handed.

A gallon of pure water weighs 10 lbs.

In Ancient Egypt princesses wore corsets made by binding cloth tightly around their waists.

There are 100,000 hairs in the average human scalp.

A tavern in Neu Isenburg, Germany, is shaped like a huge pitcher.

The real Robinson Crusoe who inspired Daniel Defoe to write his famous book, was a Scottish sailor, Alexander Selkirk, who had spent over four years alone on a desert island in the Pacific.

Noel Coward wrote one of his most successful comedies, Hay Fever, in three days.

So many languages are spoken in India that many Indians from one part of the country cannot understand their fellow countrymen from another part.

In Havana, Cuba there is a theatre called the 'Chaplin' which has a greater seating capacity than any other theatre in the world – 6,500 seats.

An Austrian walked 1,400 kilometres on his hands. He did 10 hours a day for 55 days.

William the Conqueror could jump on to a saddled horse wearing full armour; he died of injuries received from a saddle pommel.

Potatoes, roses, honeysuckle and many familiar flowers grow profusely a long way north of the Arctic Circle.

The hoatzin bird, found in South America, has a head like a small donkey.

A female elephant will always adopt a baby elephant who has lost its mother.

Muhammad is the most common first name in the world.

Sir Donald Bradman had a batting average of 99.94 runs in fifty-two Test Matches spanning twenty years.

In 1963 the Soviet newspaper 'Izvestiya' reported that a blindfolded girl had such sensitive touch that she could identify colours by feeling them.

The secretary-bird can swallow a hen's egg whole without breaking the shell.

The earliest public library is that of Kirkwall, Orkney Islands, founded in 1683.

The most prolific writer of whom there is a record is Charles Hamilton, alias Frank Richards, who created Billy Bunter. His lifetime output totalled 100,000,000 words.

The longest place name is that of the Welsh village called Llanfairpwllgwyngyllgogerychwyrnd robwllllantisiliogogoch, (known as Llanfair Pg.)

Muhammad Ali is the only man to have twice regained the World Heavyweight boxing title.

The human stomach can stretch to hold 2 pints of liquid.

The Chinese words Kung Fu mean 'leisure time'.

Caviar is 30 per cent protein.

The Basque word for God is 'Jingo'.

In the Buddhist temple at Nara in Japan there is a statue of Buddha that was cast over 1200 years ago. It weighs 452 tons – and is the largest bronze statue in the world.

A Brisbane (Australian) woman was eating an oyster when she bit on a pearl 7 mm in diameter.

The eggs of the female Goeldi's frog of South America are held on her back in folds of skin.

The shoes worn by Australian aborigines have soles made of emu feathers which leave no tracks.

Edward VII used to weigh his guests after week-ends at Sandringham to ensure that they had eaten well.

'I cry that I sin' is an anagram of 'Christianity'.

The barn owl has a night vision 2–5 times greater than a human being's.

Mark Twain made a fortune as a writer but lost it as an unsuccessful inventor.

A Hindu cannot be expelled from his religion no matter what he does in his lifetime.

The Dead Sea is actually a lake 45 miles long and 10 miles wide. This salt body of water is 1,300 feet below sea level and is the lowest spot on the surface of the earth.

There are an estimated 4,600,000 cats in Britain (100,000 of them 'employed by the Civil Service.)

Ned Kelly, an Australian highwayman, executed in 1880, always wore a suit of armour beaten out of ploughshares.

Indian women of the San Blas tribe of Panama, paint black lines on their noses to make them appear longer.

The citizens of Uruguay eat more meat per person than any other nation. They average nearly 11 lbs each per day.

Beethoven composed three sonatas when he was thirteen.

A Belgian pulled a 36 ton train along rails with his teeth.

The game of tennis originated in French monasteries in the year 1050 A.D.

Hetty Green of New York left £19 million when she died in 1916, but was so mean she saved pieces of soap in a tin and lived on cold porridge because she was too miserly to heat it.

During the Indian Mutiny the British wrote secret messages in a mixture of lemon juice and milk.

Dogs sweat through their paws.

The bellringer of Mazatlan Cathedral, Mexico, has never left the bell tower since he started work there 16 years ago.

Ainu women of Japan always cover their mouth with one hand when speaking to a man.

Prince Charles became eligible to sit in the House of Lords at the age of three, when he was made Duke of Cornwall.

George V collected 325 albums full of stamps during his lifetime.

William Penn the Quaker who founded Pennsylvania, suggested the formation of a United Nations 283 years ago.

A 5 year-old Texan boy playing his first round of golf, made a 103-yard hole-in-one.

The only food eaten by a German nun in thirty-five years was the holy wafer taken at morning mass.

Skateboard champions reach speeds of over 56 mph.

Babies can breathe and swallow at the same time – adults cannot.

In the middle ages, cooked peacock was a great delicacy.

In the Tahiti botanical Gardens, there is a bamboo plant standing 140 feet high.

The Mongol leader Kubla Khan invented the first gunpowder-filled hand-grenade in 1230.

The least number of babies are born in the countries of North, West and Central Europe. The highest birth rates are in Latin America, Africa, and Asia.

On the island of Stromboli there is an active volcano on which flocks of birds have made their home, 3,000 feet up.

Girls attending the Smolny Institute in Russia in the early twentieth century, were kept in seclusion for 7 years and not even allowed to see their own families.

The Royal Poinciana, a tropical tree, produces its flowers before it bears leaves.

The centre of the earth is almost 4000 miles beneath our feet.

The St Charles Hotel, New Orleans was destroyed by fire in 1851, as was a second hotel of the same name, on the same site 43 years later.

Eighty-five per cent of India's 625,820,000 people live in rural communities of less than 5000 inhabitants.

In 1450 an alchemist thought he had discovered the secret of making gold. He slowly cooked 2,000 egg yolks, and mixed them with olive oil and vitriol, but all it did was poison his pigs.

A balloon in which three Swedish explorers set off from Spitzbergen to the North Pole in 1897 was found 33 years later perfectly preserved in the Arctic Ice.

A temperature of minus 90.4 Fahrenheit has been recorded in Oymyakon, a town in Eastern Siberia.

There are more than 1,000,000 inhabitants in Lagos, the capital of Nigeria, which makes it the largest all-black city in the world.

Conkers are sometimes fed to cattle and horses in East Anglia, but pigs will not eat them.

In 1896 there was a war between Britain and Zanzibar which lasted thirty-eight minutes.

A modern bridge erected near Canicade, Portugal, was built over a 1700-year old Roman bridge.

The hogshead became the standard measure for the liquids in 1423.

There is more copper in the brain and liver of a baby than in those of an adult.

One-quarter of the world's cattle live in India.

Nine out of ten Indian girls are married by the time they reach twenty.

King Gustav III of Sweden ordered a convicted murderer to drink himself to death with coffee. The king believed coffee to be poisonous, but the murderer proved that it was not.

The horned toad looks ferocious, but has a mild disposition and makes a good pet.

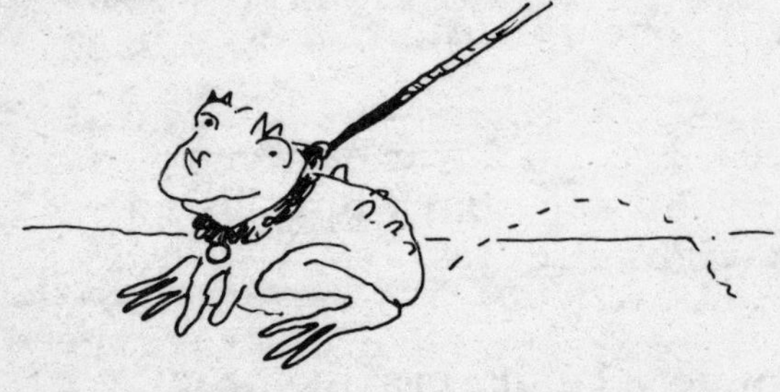

A tortoise which died in 1966 was over 200 years old. It was presented to the King of Tonga in 1773 by Captain Cook.

Sneezing was a favourable omen in the ancient world.

The Emperor Napoleon was terrified of cats.

A New Yorker was so expert at forging signatures that he was hired to sign the names of 250,000 celebrities.

A butterfly can look at you through 12,000 eyes.

William Henry Vanderbilt the richest man in the world at his death in 1885, was buried in a mausoleum which was inspected by a watchman every 15 minutes to make sure his corpse was not kidnapped.

The Chinese knew about differential gearing before the birth of Christ.

The Osaka-Okayama Express in Japan travels at an average speed of 103 mph.

5,000 old tyres are to be used to build an artificial reef as a shelter for fish at St Vincent's Gulf in South Australia.

The steel interior skeleton of the Statue of Liberty was designed by Alexandre Gustave Eiffel, who designed the Eiffel Tower in Paris.

In London in the 1800s used sets of false teeth were advertised for sale.

Wealthy women in seventeenth century Russia wore pearl-studded hats to hide their heads, which were shaved at their marriage ceremony.

A hotel in Tokyo has a solid gold bath and charges visitors 1,000 yen for a 2-minute dip. They believe it will add 3 years to the bather's life.

The skull of a Stone Age man, estimated at 40,000 years old, was found in Zambia in 1921.

In 1221 the army of Genghis Khan massacred 1,748,000 people at Nishapur, north-eastern Iran, in one hour.

New York was originally discovered by a Florentine sailor, Giovanni Varrazoni, in 1524.

The gestation period of a rhinoceros is 560 days.

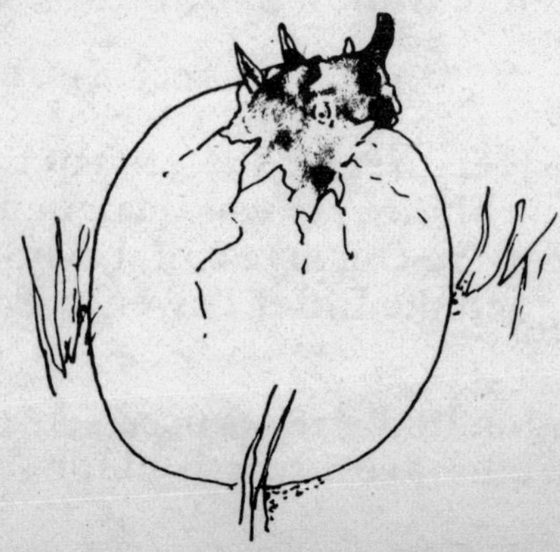

The earth is $5\frac{1}{2}$ times denser than water.

Because her face had sunk inwards after the loss of her front teeth, Queen Elizabeth I used to appear in public with her mouth stuffed with fine cloth.

The greatest recorded temperature variation in one day occurred at Browning, Montana, USA on 23rd–24th January 1916, when the temperature fell from 44°F to –56°F.

When the River Arno flooded Florence in 1966, it caused damage estimated at £57 million to the city's art treasures.

A Polish mathematical wizard was employed by his government to replace 40 trained men and 40 calculating machines.

Don Quixote has been more widely translated than any other book with the exception of the Bible.

Red squirrels attract more fleas than other animals.

In 1972 a London boy scout tossed a pancake 2,105 times.

Many people believe that warm water freezes sooner than cold water. It does not.

Flocks of migrating cranes will sometimes hold a dance before flying. They bow to each other before beginning their dance.

A Rhodesian man shooting from 37 metres scored a 'gold' with his first arrow; his second arrow split the first one and both arrows finished in a staight line.

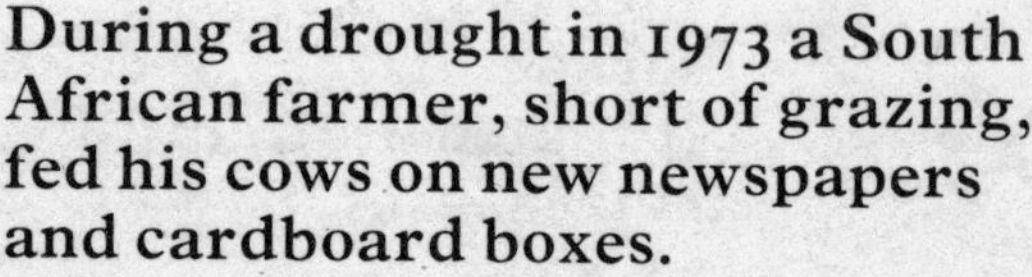

During a drought in 1973 a South African farmer, short of grazing, fed his cows on new newspapers and cardboard boxes.

In Switzerland there are more than 1,000 lakes.

A Holy man in Benares, India, has held his left arm in the same position for 12 years.

Henry M. Stanley, the American journalist who found David Livingstone in Africa, during the Civil War served with both the Confederate Army and the Union Navy.

The smallest plane to fly was owned by a Californian and was 9 feet 10 inches long. It could fly at up to 185 mph.

The midnight sun ensures that there is constant daylight for 24 hours each day for 73 consecutive days in northern Finland.

A cow grazing on one acre of pasture will produce over one tonne of milk a year.

Lunar eclipses only occur during a full moon. There are never more than three lunar eclipses in a year.

Our nearest star neighbour is 40,232,500 km (25 million miles) away.

The interior of Greenland consists of an immense mass of ice, where nothing grows.

Lucrezia Borgia was married four times before she was twenty-two.

The longest snake is the reticulated python of Southeast Asia, which regularly exceeds 20 feet in length.

The Swedes are the world's greatest coffee drinkers and consume over 29 lbs of coffee per person a year.

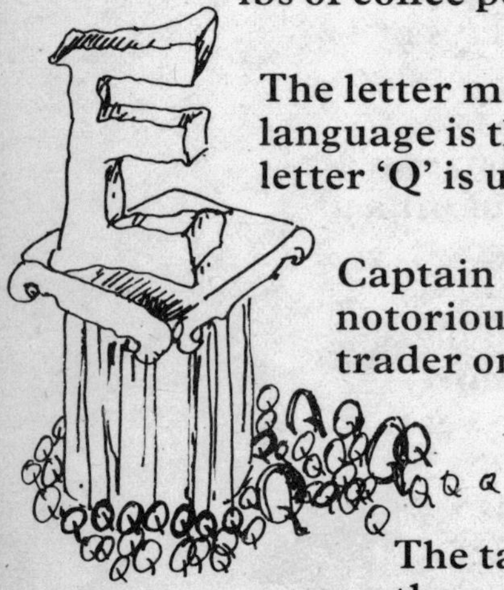

The letter most in use in the English language is the letter 'E' and the letter 'Q' is used the least.

Captain Kidd, before he became a notorious pirate was a respected trader on New York's Wall Street.

The tallest people in the world are the men of the Watutsi tribe of Central Africa, who are often 2.3 metres tall.

The Church of Sompting in England is the only one in the country with a gabled roof.

Contrary to popular belief alcohol does not warm the body but reduces body heat rapidly.

Shredded wheat was the first breakfast cereal, and was introduced in Colorado in 1893.

Until 1879 British soldiers convicted of bad conduct were tattooed with the initials 'B.C.'

Many eighteenth century women went to the lengths of having their gums pierced in order to keep their dentures in place with hooks.

In the USSR a citizen is not allowed to own land, but can build his own house, and this may be inherited by his heirs after his death.

An American circus performer was able to increase his stature from 5 feet 10 ins to 6 feet 4 inches, at will.

The Emperor Penguin of the Antarctic can reach a depth of 870 feet and remain submerged for as long as 18 minutes.

In Upper Austria there is a monument called the Pillar of Death were 300 men, women and children stricken in the plague of 1620 gathered to await death.

Women of Zeeland Province, Netherlands, wear bonnets that indicate their religion.

All Sikhs are called 'Singh', meaning 'lion hearted'.

In Westphalia, Germany you could buy at least 400 varieties of sausage.

Holland has the densest population per square mile of any nation on the world.

The poet Geoffrey Chaucer was the first person to be buried in Poets' Corner, Westminster Abbey.

The diameter of the earth's orbit is almost exactly 1000 times the distance that the light travels in one second.

Immanual Nobel, father of Alfred Nobel, the inventor of gunpowder, himself invented plywood.

In 1962 an American swam from France to England underwater in 18 hours.

There is an archipelago in S.W. Finland which has 30,000 islands.

A Rhode Island portrait artist painted 1,000 portraits of herself.

The Battle of Hastings was fought on King Harold's birthday.

Popocatepétl is the name of a 17,000 foot high volcano in Mexico. The last time it erupted was in 1702.

'Purdah' is the Islamic custom of keeping women secluded, and many Moslem women in Pakistan wear the 'burqa', an ankle-length garment with slits for the eyes.

An Italian mathematician, Paolo Dagomari, conceived the idea of using the comma to separate large figures into units of three, in the 14th century.

In 1971 two American youths in Manassa, see-sawed non-stop for 200 hours.

Until this century the world ivory market greatly relied on the tusks of prehistoric mammoths found in north-eastern Siberia.

Henry V was only fifteen when he fought at the Battle of Shrewsbury in 1403.

'Dead as the dodo' – the dodo was a bird found on the Island of Mauritius. They were killed for food by the sailors, and the last one died in 1681.

A wingless orthopteran insect can survive in a frozen state in the Arctic for months, but dies if exposed to the warmth of a human hand.

Buhram, a member of the violent Indian Thugee sect, strangled over 900 people in fifty years.

Much of the barley to make Scotch whisky is imported into Scotland from California, Canada, India and Africa.

For several years after the Second World War stores in Japan wooed American customers by signs which read 'Forgive and Forget'.

Though only 23 cm long the squeaker, or trident fish, can kill crocodiles.

Anne Boleyn, second wife of Henry VIII, had an extra finger on her left hand.

In 1785 Louis XVI issued a decree that all handkerchiefs must be square.

A dragonfly has been known to eat forty house-flies in less than two hours.

Many perfumes are compounded of a substance produced in the glands of the civet, a cat-like animal found in Ethiopia.

PERFUME À LA CAT

Mary Queen of Scots was a skilful billiards player.

An anagram of 'French Revolution' is 'violence run forth'.

Just before Christmas 1931 an Australian ordered a new two-piece suit. From the fleece on the sheep's back it was transformed into the finished article in 1 hour 52 minutes 18.5 seconds.

There are reported to be more ghosts per square mile in Britain than in any other country.

It is not unusual to see a woman smoking a cigar in Denmark.

The entire contents of the first gramophone record was: 'Mary had a little lamb'.

'Typhoid Mary' was the name given to Mary Mallon of New York City who was responsible for 1,300 cases of typhoid. She was eventually placed under permanent detention from 1915 until her death in 1938.

The rickshaw was invented by an American Baptist minister in Japan in 1888.

By the end of 1976 over 185 million bottles of Coca-Cola were bought every day.

William III, Queen Anne, George I, George II, George III and George IV all died on Saturdays.

The average summer temperature of the Red Sea is 35°C.

The first time Christopher Columbus ever set foot on mainland America was on his third voyage in 1498. This was in Venezuela, at a point called Cristobal Colon.

On the Island of Rhodes there is a place called 'The Valley of the Butterflies' where thousands of butterflies are attracted and are so thick that they darken the landscape.

Four English boy scouts shined 707 pairs of shoes in 18 hours.

The first motor cycle was invented by Gottlieb Daimler in Germany in 1885.

The Red Jacket, a clipper sailing from New York to Liverpool crossed the Atlantic in 13 days in 1854, and set a speed record that was never broken.

Amy Semple MacPherson, an American spiritualist and evangelist, was buried with a live telephone in her coffin.

RING .... RING... RING. RING... RING... R.I.P.

In 1940 338,226 British and French troops were evacuated from Dunkirk.

The monkey's dinner bell is a South American nut that explodes when it is ripe.

In Macedonia, Yugoslavia fishermen use trained birds to catch fish. There is a band around the neck of the bird so that it can't swallow the fish. It returns with the catch, and the fisherman removes the fish!

Workers in Japanese silk factories cook and eat the grubs they find inside the cocoons of silkworms.

In a churchyard near Oaxara, in Mexico, there is an *ahuehuete* tree, whose trunk is 160 feet in circumference. It is believed to be one of the oldest living things on the American continent.

One town in the United States – Braintree, Massachusetts, has produced two Presidents. They are John Adams, and his son, John Quincy Adams.

John Logie Baird demonstrated television in public for the first time in 1926; the first television broadcasting station was opened at Alexandra Palace in London ten years later.

Ahmed Zog I of Albania achieved the dubious distinction of smoking 240 cigarettes a day.

Some homes in Catalonia, Spain, have palm branches attached to them, as the inhabitants believe this will protect them from lightning.

A sergeant of the Japanese Army hid in the jungles of Guam for 28 years rather then surrender after Japan's defeat in World War II.

As the earth whirls round on its axis a spot on the Equator moves at over 1000 mph.

Written English contains 10,000 words but the better educated person uses no more than 5,000 words when speaking.

The belfry of the church of Kippen, Scotland, is the only part of the structure still standing, and is covered with centuries of ivy.

The sword used by King Edward III required two ordinary men to lift it.

The Eastree Lookout in Western Australia is climbed by a spiral ladder. The cabin is 61 metres high and gives a view over the state forest to watch for fires.

It is possible to sail all the way round the earth on latitude 60°south.

In 1972 the defence budget of Andorra was the equivalent of £2.00.

The most popular recreational activities in the United States are boating and fishing. Bowling and hunting come next.

In Brazil there is a rodent called the agouti, almost as big as a rabbit, which is caught and eaten for food.

The earliest English comedy was written by the headmaster of Eton and performed by his pupils in 1553. It was called Ralph Royster Doyster.

The panama hat is made from the undeveloped leaves of the stemless screw-pine, and has nothing to do with Panama.

The old Grand Central Station in New York City was kept clean by a strictly enforced rule that passenger trains had to be coasted in without engines.

In November 1872 the brigantine 'Mary Celeste' was found sailing in mid-Atlantic. Breakfast had been cooked but not eaten, everything was in order and the lifeboat intact. There was no sign of a struggle or of a storm, but the 12-man crew had disappeared.

The average medieval man was only 5 ft. 6 ins tall.

Every verse of Psalm 136 ends with the same words.

During the first Battle of the Somme in 1916 the sound of the gunfire could be heard on Hampstead Heath.

Sarah Bernhardt, famous nineteenth century actress, frequently slept in a rosewood coffin.

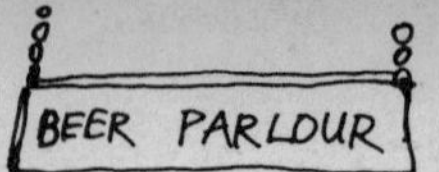

In Saskatchewan, Canada, it is illegal to drink water in beer parlours.

A kangaroo can hop at an estimated speed of 41 km per hour.

Indian tribes of the N.W. coast of America used copper shields for money.

The Ashanti Campaign in Africa was the last occasion in which British troops fought in scarlet uniforms.

When it is 1.00 p.m. in Moscow the time is 10.00 p.m. in Anadyr at the other end of the USSR.

The Virginia home of Thomas Jefferson has only two very narrow staircases because Jefferson considered them a waste of space.

A husband in Morocco can divorce his wife simply by saying 'I divorce thee' three times.

Ten times as many men as women are colour blind.

The first time an equals sign (=) was used was in an algebra text in 1557.

Oliver Morosco, the Broadway producer, made more than $5,000,000 from his hit shows but when he died at 69 he had only 8 cents in his pocket.

Sir Winston Churchill's last words were: 'Oh, I am so bored with it all.'

A swarm of locusts crossed the Red Sea in 1889, which covered an area 5,180 sq. km, and must have weighed 500,000 tons.

There are over 500 characters in Tolstoy's War and Peace.

In 1861 Charles Blondin, the famous acrobat, turned a back somersault on stilts 170 feet above the ground without a safety-net.

The word 'karate' means 'empty hand'.

It was estimated that 4 million people thronged Cairo, Egypt, for the funeral of President Nasser, on October 1, 1970.

In 1976 an Englishman managed to walk 12 yards on stilts 22 feet 9 inches high.

The narrowest street in the world is in Port Isaac, Cornwall, where it is popularly known as 'Squeeze-Belly Alley'.

Rodrigo Borgia was the father of at least four children before being elected Pope Alexander VI in 1492.

The living are outnumbered by the dead on earth by roughly thirty to one.

In World War II it is estimated that the total number of fatalities including battle deaths and civilians of all countries was 54,800,000, the costliest war in history.

There are at least 100,000 million stars in the Milky Way.

Lawn tennis originated from a game played by French monks in monastery cloisters in the eleventh century.

Frederick the Great used to have his veins opened in battle as he believed it helped to calm his nerves.

In eight years at the beginning of the seventeenth century 2,000 French aristocrats were killed fighting duels.

St Paul's Gate, Verdun, France has an inscription which reads, 'Verdun, destroyed in 10 months, February to December 1916. Rebuilt in 10 years, 1919–1929'.

A bottle containing a message dropped in the Pacific Ocean in 1947 came to land at Sylt in the North Sea in 1968. It had travelled over 125,000 miles.

During his reign Charles II 'touched' almost 100,000 sufferers from scrofula who believed the king's touch would cure them.

The church of Tscherniheim, Carinthia, Austria, is the only structure standing in the village deserted by all its inhabitants nearly 100 years ago.

Queen Victoria was a carrier of classical haemophilia (a disease carried to male offspring which prevented clotting of the blood).

William Shakespeare had red hair.

In the Great Fire of London in 1666 only six people died.

Honey used to be given to babies during baptism.

In the Wankie National Park in Rhodesia there is a herd of 4,000 elephants.

Hadrian's Wall in the north of England is 77 miles long.

The mean annual temperature in Reykjavik, just below the Arctic Circle, is higher than that in New York.

The organ of the Anglican Cathedral in Liverpool has over 9700 pipes.

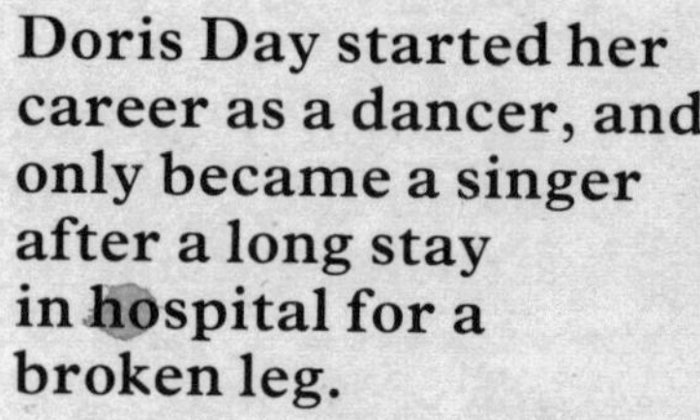

Doris Day started her career as a dancer, and only became a singer after a long stay in hospital for a broken leg.

Nearly 40 per cent of the USSR is covered by forests.

Tennyson wrote a 60000-word poem when he was ten.

During the reign of Peter the Great in Russia a special tax was levied on beards.

James Gordon Bennett, the newspaper editor who sent Stanley to Africa to find Livingstone, was convinced he would not live beyond his his 77th birthday. He sank into a coma on his 77th birthday, and died 4 days later.

The coal mined in Britain was formed 270–300 million years ago.

The fifth satellite of Uranus was only discovered in 1948.

Football was first played in England in the twelfth century but no rules were devised until 1846.

The earth is roughly 4600 million years old.

War galleys powered by slaves were still in use during the reign of Louis XIV in the seventeenth century.

Pope Paul III decreed slavery for all Englishmen who supported Henry VIII.

In Haiti peasants wear printed Christian prayers on a string as a protection against evil.

Salt was once a very precious commodity, so much so that many people were paid their wages in salt – hence the word 'salary'.

The first atomic submarine Nautilus was launched in 1954.

The Sahara is as large as Europe and larger than the combined area of the next nine largest deserts in the world.

Strings of beads are still used by the Kayan tribe of Borneo as money.

Up to 30,000 tonnes of cosmic dust are deposited on the earth each year.

Mothers who smoke produce lighter babies than mothers who do not.

On the island of Euboea in the Aegean there is a channel of water which mystifies scientists. The current actually reverses its direction 14 times every day.

The long-tailed fowl of Kochi, Japan, have tails more than 20 feet long.

During the Second World War a rocket fell through the roof of the British Museum, passing through a hole made by a previous rocket – both of them failed to explode when they hit the building.

Magnetic north is 1500 miles west of the North Pole.

Ice-hockey pucks shoot across the ice at nearly 112 mph.

The sacred ibis was believed by the Ancient Egyptians to be the bird that hatched the 'world egg'.

The Japanese spider crab has legs which can span over 12 feet.

In a planetarium in New York City there is a meteorite weighing over 34 tons.

Elvis Presley earned a record 37 golden discs.

The Black Death in the fourteenth century resulted in an estimated 75 million deaths.

The Potter Wasp makes a vase-like nest of clay. It then hangs the egg inside on a thread and the 'vase' is stocked with a caterpillar on which the larva will feed.

Pope Benedict IX became Pope when he was twelve, but was later expelled for vice and moral corruption.

A Park Ranger of Virginia, USA, has been struck by lightning seven times.

The train journey from Moscow to Vladivostok in the USSR is 6000 miles long and takes nine days.

As recently as 1923 the mortality rate among horse drivers in England and Wales was over 60 per cent higher than that among motor vehicle drivers.

The Rhaetian Railway in Switzerland is 245 miles long and traverses 488 bridges and 119 tunnels.

At Knossos, on the island of Crete, there are the ruins of a palace built 4,000 years ago, which contains complete bathrooms, with modern-style drainage systems.

An eighteenth century London woman was so afraid of catching cold that she never washed, but lubricated her face and hands with lard. She lived to be 116.

Herons have special combs on their toes for scratching off slime from fish. They also treat their feathers with powder produced by special feathers on the body.

A ram adds an additional spiral section to its horns every year.

The southernmost manned lighthouse in the world is Cape Pembroke Lighthouse in the Falkland Islands.

The official cause of death of George IV was listed as rupture of the stomach blood vessels, alcoholic cirrhosis, gout, nephritis and dropsy.

The bayonet is named after the French town Bayonne.

Milan cathedral took 579 years to build and seats a congregation of 40,000.

The official name for Libya is 'Splaj', the Socialist People's Libyan Arab Jamahiriya.

The archer fish can hit an insect up to 122 cm away with drops of water squirted from its mouth.

It takes 5 tons of rock to produce a piece of gold the size of a trouser button.

The nineteenth chapter of the Second Book of Kings and the thirty-seventh chapter of Isaiah are almost identical.

Following one of his victories the fourteenth-century Turkish chief Tamerlane built 120 pyramids containing the heads of 80,000 of the defeated enemy.

Oliver Cromwell won two important battles on September 3rd – those of Worcester and Dunbar. He also died on September 3rd, 1658.

When the Hong Kong Jockey Club racecourse collapsed and caught fire in February 1918, 604 people were killed.

Nadia Comaneci, a 14-year-old Rumanian gymnast, received 7 perfect marks in the 1976 Olympics.

The largest non-Christian religion is Islam (Muslim) with about 550,000,000 followers.

The first adhesive postage stamps (the Penny Blacks) came into use in England on May 6, 1840.

A Doberman dog once tracked a stock thief 100 miles by scent alone across the Great Karroo, South Africa.

Flies take off with a backward jump.

A half-breed fox terrier living in Sydney, Australia hates cats and has killed ten, but has kidnapped a ginger kitten and looks after it like a puppy and won't give it up to its mother.

Before 1920 it was rare for trucks to move faster than 10 mph.

Pepi II was Pharoah in Egypt for ninety-four years.

In 1958 Joy Foster became the table-tennis singles and mixed-doubles champion of Jamaica when she was eight.

A mole can dig a tunnel 100 yards long in a single night.

Rasputin 'the mad monk' was finally drowned after he had survived frequent attempts to poison him. To make sure he was dead he was also beaten with an iron bar and shot twice.

Water is still brought to the town of Segovia in Spain by an aqueduct built in A.D. 110 by the Romans.

The modern jury system was originated by William the Conqueror who set up juries of 12 men in each district to assure honest tax payments.

Women of the Jos Plateau, Togoland, Africa, make known their married status by wearing a small bustle of plaited straw.

In Chaouen, in Northern Morocco you can see snow on trees and rooftops during the summer.

Before evolving his theory of relativity, Albert Einstein had worked as a clerk in a patents office.

The paradise fish of Thailand builds its nest underwater, bringing air from the surface and saliva to create a nest of bubbles.

Fireflies are bright enough to shine through the stomach of a frog.

Half the words denoting trickery and deceit in the English language are derived from playing cards.

The only flying mammals are bats, the largest of which is the Kalong found in Malaysia and Indonesia, which has a wing span of up to 5 feet 7 inches.

The Forest of Martyrs near Jerusalem has 6 million trees – each tree being a memorial to a Jewish life lost in Nazi Europe.

Anti-conscription riots occurred in New York in 1863, in which 1200 people were killed.

Rubber is used in the manufacture of bubble-gum; it is the substance that makes blowing the bubble possible.

An Australian gold-miner in 1869 found a nugget weighing 142 pounds.

On the Cotentin Peninsula of France flowers bloom in profusion on the thatched roofs of farm buildings.

In most Dutch cities you can see herring stalls. The Dutch love to eat them there on the streets.

Eighty per cent of the world's supply of dates come from Iraq.

When Westminster Abbey was built its congregation numbered less than sixty.

Bulimia is a rare disease which causes sufferers to spend as much as 15 hours a day eating.

A portable dressing-tent for bathers, was sold in England in the 1920s, supported by a top shaped like a lampshade, that rested on the bather's head.

The chewing of fresh parsley will take away the smell of garlic.

During the Second World War nearly 649,000 jeeps were manufactured.

The Roman Emperor Caligula made his horse a consul.

A bridge built by the Incas across the Apurimac River in Peru in 1350 and spanning a 150 feet gap was in use for more than 500 years.

The first Black American to hold an elective office was John Mercer Langston (1829–1897). He was born a slave and became town clerk in Lorain County, Ohio in 1845.

There are an estimated 5,000,000 sheep in Wales.

A chamber-pot full of salt used to be a common wedding present in north-east Scotland.

Mortgages were being provided by Babylonian banks in 2100 B.C.

It takes $2\frac{1}{2}$ pounds of grain to produce a pound of chicken meat, 3 lbs of grain for each pound of pork and 10 pounds of grain for a pound of beef.

The world's only living prehistoric lizards can be found on the island of Komodo, Indonesia, and reach 10 feet in length.

Scientists have found that mice prefer women to men.

A Florida, US, man has the largest pair of shoes ever made. They are 60 cm long and 30 cm wide.

The Stone Mosque in Iran, is carved out of solid rock, and was a Christian church until 1254.

The Cathedral of Rome, is St John Lateran, not St Peter's.

Nelson's flagship HMS Victory carried a crew of 850.

The dugongs, sometimes called 'sea cows' are two metres long, live on seaweed, and first gave rise to the mermaid myth.

The Egyptians were the first to calculate the solar year with 365 days.

A Stroud (Gloustershire) man threw a standard brick 42.26 metres in 1970.

The meat of the hippopotamus though not normally eaten for food, is said to taste like juicy pork or veal.

There is a sport popular in Austria called 'ski-joring' which is a land equivalent of water-skiing. The skiers are pulled across snow-covered roads by riders on horseback.

The oldest pharmacy in Europe is still in use today in Dubrovnik, Yugoslavia, which opened in 1317. They also opened an Old People's Home in 1347, and a medical service in 1301.

Natives of New Guinea often smoke their home-made cigarettes from the side.

Thousands of sheep were killed by an ice bombardment in Texas in 1877.

The civilizations of the Aztecs, Toltecs, Incas and Mayans all functioned without the wheel.

The author of the most influential book in English law, Sir William Blackstone, never practiced law himself.

The first recorded Olympic Games took place in 776 B.C. and consisted of a 200 yards foot race.

A 13-year-old Tasmanian girl proved that an earthworm can pull 10 times its own weight.

In 1949 the hair of the head of the Thuravadu-Thurai Monastery in India, was 8 metres long.

Outside the United States, Australia has the largest number of NASA space tracking and communication establishments in the world.

Prime Minister of Britain, W. E. Gladstone, used to chew each mouthful of food thirty-two times.

A Parisian chef, Nicholas Appert, in 1809 discovered practical way of preserving food in glass jars sealed with corks.

The first mechanical clock was invented in China in A.D. 725.

Sir Francis Drake captured booty worth £600,000 on his voyage of 1580, which represented a return of 4700 per cent to his investors on their capital.

The Hapsburg family kept the title of Holy Roman Emperor from 1273 until 1806, when they became the Emperors of Austria until 1918.

The world's smallest trophy, was presented to the President of the International Governing body of swimming, and was made from a gold thimble and a collar button; it is only one inch high.

Henry III inherited the throne when he was only ten months old.

The death penalty is still in force in Britain for those convicted of high treason or piracy with violence.

The word 'tip' is an abbreviation of 'To Insure Promptness'.

The typing exercise 'The quick brown fox jumps over the lazy dog' contains all the letters of the alphabet.

There are no roads in the City of London. Every road turns into a street when it reaches the City.

The twenty-six letters of our alphabet can be transposed 620,448,401,733,239,439,369,000 times.

The Okavango River carries 26% more water than all the rivers of South Africa combined, yet none of it is discharged into the sea.

If your tongue were quite dry, you wouldn't be able to taste anything.

The entire Mongol nation which conquered all of northern Asia and China in the thirteenth century numbered no more than about one million people.

The Pedaung woman of Burma stretch their necks with large numbers of brass rings.

After birth the volume of the body increases twenty times or more, but the eyes only increase three and a quarter times in size.

Three-quarters of all Norwegian people live within 10 miles of the sea.

A goose is faithful to its mate all its life.

Nobody, not even the Prime Minister, has a key to Number 10 Downing Street – the door only opens from the inside.

One of the best ways to clean your teeth is by chewing on a stick.

There are over 10 million people who share your birthday.

In twenty-four hours the average healthy adult breathes 23,000 times.

A man of Newport Beach, California, wears a lapel pin showing two pearls he found in a bowl of oyster stew.

The Arctic tern flies from the Arctic round the world to the Antarctic and back again every year.

All the female eggs needed to produce the next generation of the human race could be contained within the shell of one chicken's egg.

If you could siphon the petrol out of one jumbo jet and put it into a minicar, you could drive four times round the world.

An elephant has 1 lb of brain for every 1000 lbs of body weight.

George III bought over 67,000 books during his lifetime.

Unlike most cities in the world Venezuela welcomes pigeons, and the city has built elegant pigeon houses everywhere for the birds to live in.

In addition to the capital of Italy, there is also a city called Rome on every continent.

In the late nineteenth century fashionable women in England achieved pink cheeks and lips and shapely eyebrows by tattooing.

In 1939 you could buy a daily paper, a packet of ten cigarettes, a half-pound bar of chocolate and a seat at the cinema for two shillings (10p.)

If you soak an egg in vinegar for a few days the shell will soften and the egg will bounce.

You may not 'whistle, sing, play a musical instrument, carry a bulky package, wheel a pram, carry an open umbrella, or run' through the Burlington Arcade, Piccadilly, London.

The Kagu bird, found on the island of New Caledonia, runs but cannot fly. It feeds on worms, and barks like a dog.

An unfaithful wife in the Tupuri tribe of Africa, must wear a brass ring around her neck for the rest of her life.

The staple diet for about one half of the population of the world is rice.

Sweden has had almost no illiteracy since 1842 since every child in Sweden has had to go to school for at least 7 years.

A dog can hear high-frequency sounds which a human ear cannot.

All mammals, except man and monkey, are colour-blind.

Twenty-one people were killed in Rhodesia when the hut in which they were sheltering was struck by lightning.

The ballpoint pen was invented by Hungarian brothers called Biro, and during the first full year on the British market, 53 million biros were sold.

Prince Philip was the first member of the Royal Family to be interviewed on television – on Panorama in 1961.

The word 'girl' occurs only once in the Bible.

Emily Dickinson, an American poet (1830–1886) considered herself so ugly that when callers came to her home she remained in another room and conversed through an open door.

Flower and Flour used to be the same word. Flour was the flower, or best part, of the wheat.

Most people can distinguish 10,000 different smells.

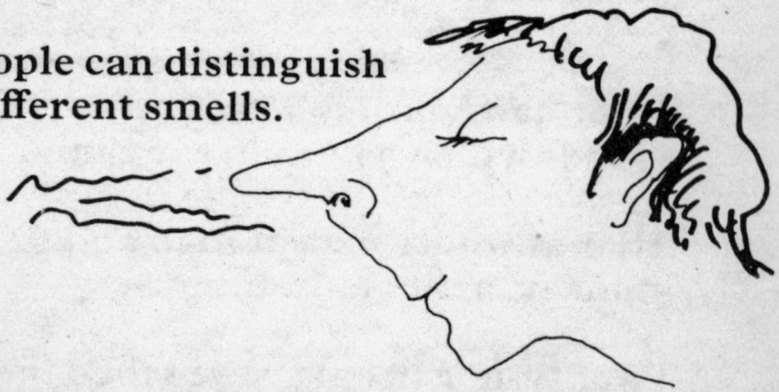

London has had only seven white Christmases since 1900.

Lake Baskunchak in the USSR is a salt-water lake that is continually fed by salt springs, and scientists estimate there is enough salt there to meet the world's needs for more than a thousand years.

A Pennsylvania (US) man simultaneously broke four blocks of ice, weighing 1,000 lbs, with his elbow.

In 1939–40 an ancient city of 800 houses was discovered in Alaska, estimated by archaeologists to be 2000 years old.

The Chinese used rockets against the Mongols in 1232.

If it's raining 'cats and dogs' in England, it's raining 'small spears' in France and 'bits of string' in Germany.

Surtsey, a natural island near Iceland, was thrown up by an underwater volcano in 1963 and now has both plant and animal life.

The trunk of the baobab tree in Kenya is so large that some natives make their homes inside the hollowed-out trunks.

The first printing press in America was set up by Stephen Day in Cambridge, Mass., in 1640.

In the Kalocsa region of Hungary an old folk-art still pertains; that is painting the whole house inside with decorations and patterns like carpets.

The stone balls often found on top of gate-posts are the relic of the gruesome custom of hanging the heads of enemies and criminals over one's gate.

The tree toad of Martinique climbs trees with its young clinging to its back.

On May 25 every year Gypsies from all over Europe meet at the town of Saintes-Maries-de-la-Mer in France.

A lock invented in the 1800s held small explosive caps and surprised a burglar by exploding with a loud bang.

A person's temperature can be chilled down to 25 degrees Centigrade without harmful effects.

The colour of mourning in China is white.

The South Head lighthouse in Australia was constructed by a convict-architect, who was pardoned for his work.

A Scottish terrier owned by a Manchester woman, swallowed a knitting needle 12 inches long. The dog itself was 15 inches long.

The Bank of England has its own water supplied by an artesian well.

William Pitt the younger became Britain's youngest Prime Minister at the age of twenty-four.

Oliver Cromwell was born and christened Oliver Williams.

The oldest bridge in Australia is that over the Coal River in Tasmania, which was built in 1823.

Little Miss Muffet was a real person. Her father was an entomologist (one who studies spiders, among other insects).

At the time when the Danes were attacking Britain, the Chinese were perfecting gun powder.

The Marianas Trench in the Pacific is nearly 7 miles deep. An object dropped over this depression would take more than an hour to sink to the bottom.

Noah Webster, who published his first dictionary in 1828, had worked for 21 years to compile its 70,000 words.

Whale songs have been recorded deep in the ocean. They range from deep roaring to falsetto singing.

Ainu girls of Japan often added a tattooed moustache to their upper lip in the belief that it made them more attractive.

Elizabeth Blackwell, the first woman doctor of modern times (she died in 1910) was opposed to vaccination.

Doubtful Sound is the name of an inlet in South Island, New Zealand.

Tumble dolls were first made by the Chinese in the image of Buddha, with weighted buttons to illustrate that Buddha could not fall.

The first woman to orbit the earth was 26-year old Valentina Tereshkova, of the USSR.

A leading New York dog delicatessen caters for pampered dogs who ride up to the private dining room for pets in chauffeured limousines.

When Beethoven was deaf he managed to 'hear' a little by placing a stick on the top of his piano and biting on it.

The male silkworm moths have a keen sense of smell and can detect a female moth more than 6 miles away.

Carrots are made into a porridge in India, a wine in Britain and a substitute for coffee in Germany.

A Wisconsin (USA) man hibernated each winter for 23 years from November to Easter.

A wren can sing 130 different notes in seven seconds.

At the equinoxes in March and September there is an equal number of hours of light and darkness everywhere on the earth.

In 1685 the average wage of an English labourer was four shillings (20p) per week.

The size of a newly-born kangaroo is 2.5 cm.

During a two-year period (1911–13) when the Mona Lisa was stolen, six Americans individually paid $300,000 for what they mistakenly believed to be the original.

A man from North Carolina enlisted in the US army at 14, served 2 years including 5 months in combat in Korea, was made a sergeant, and then discharged as under age.

'School' comes from the Greek word skhole which means 'leisure'.

Dostoievsky, the famous Russian writer, was sentenced to death for political conspiracy, and was reprieved by an order from the Czar when he was on the scaffold.

An anagram of 'astronomers' is 'moon starers.'

The sun's corona comes into view during a total eclipse.

Baobob trees found in the tropics, have trunks 30 feet in diameter.

The soles of a cat's paws will perspire if it hears a dog barking.

The Winston Churchill Memorial and Library in Fulton, Mass., US, was built from the stones of the Church of St Mary in Aldermanbury, London, burned and razed by bombs in World War II.

An underpass crosses the M5 motorway at Exeter, made especially for badgers; it is 30 cm wide.

During the reign of Charles II the fashionable place for the young men to show off their fine clothes was in the aisle of old St Paul's Cathedral

Chinese comic books are very popular with children in Hong Kong but as few of them can afford to buy them, there are street stands where the comics can be hired cheaply and they sit there and read them.

Gravity on the surface of the star Sirius is 250,000 times greater than the earth's gravity.

The Royal Mails were started by Charles I and the person who received the letter had to pay for it.

In Tudor times all four-poster beds had curtains to pull round at night – this was because the houses had no upstairs corridors and people had to go through one room to get to another, hence the need for privacy in bed.

A Leicester lady worked for 86 years with the same elastic company. She began at the age of 9 and was still working at 95.

You can see the stars from the bottom of a well even in daylight.

The first stretch of motorway to be opened in Britain was near Preston, Lancashire, in 1958.

Ice-cream made from frozen milk, was on sale in Peking during Marco Polo's visit.

St Nicholas is the patron saint of thieves.

A prison in Athens in which Socrates was imprisoned is still standing more than 2,375 years later.

When a man was being hanged in Mississippi in 1894 the noose came undone and the prisoner fell to the ground. He was then set free, and since his innocence was later established he was granted $5,000.

A New Haven, Connecticut, man lived to the age of 83 after surviving 28 narrow escapes from death.

The famous 'Siamese' twins, Chang and Eng Bunker born in May 1811, were joined at the chest. They married sisters, and died, within three hours of each other, in January 1874.

The first coach to be used in England was presented to Elizabeth I by a Dutchman in 1565.

While fishing in Pittwater, new South Wales, a man caught a new fishing rod, reel and tackle.

The greatest live weight for a turkey is 75 lbs reported in 1973 for a turkey reared in Salt Lake City.

During the time of Chaucer it was against the law to store Spanish wine and French wine in the same cellar.

The idea of Santa Claus as we know him today was designed by a 19th century American artist. Hitherto he was always pictured as a bishop in his vestments.

After his escape from a prisoner-of-war camp in the Boer War in 1899, Winston Churchill had a £25 reward, dead or alive placed on his head.

Turtles have no teeth.

Blood takes one minute to be pumped round the body and return to the heart.

The Americans drink 411,200 million gallons of water a day.

A French monk (1539–1609) ate only one meal a day for 48 years, consisting of bread, water and a few raw roots.

An orange weighing 3 lbs 11 oz was grown by a native of Tucson, Arizona in 1977.

Registration plates for motor cars were introduced into Britain in 1903 and the original A1 plate was obtained by the 2nd Earl Russell for his 12 hp Napier.

There are more than 600 muscles in our muscular system.

The deep sea angler fish has a glowing rod over its mouth. Small fish are attracted by the light and snapped up by the sharp teeth.

Skyscraper nests built by magnetic ants are only found in Northern Australia, and the ants are so named because their nests always point north and south.

The Great Fire of London (1666) burned down 85 churches including old St Paul's, and hundreds of fine buildings. It also destroyed the filthy alleys and narrow streets cleansing the town of all traces of the plague from the previous year.

The Indian Atlas moth has a wing span of 11 ins.

The longest chair lift in the world is above Thredbo, New South Wales, Australia. It takes from 45 to 75 minutes to ascend the 3 miles depending on the weather.

In Poland the goat is considered to herald good fortune, while the crow, wolf and pigeon are considered unlucky.

Moths do not eat clothes. It is their larvae that do the damage.

The church of St Andrews in Singapore, is a replica of the Abbey of Netley, England, and was built in 1861 by convicts.

The first man executed in an electric chair took eight minutes to die.

The black widow spider, contrary to popular belief, is timid and only bites when molested. If hungry the female will eat her mate, which is how she got her name.

The Babylonian zero was written like a modern colon (:).

An eighteenth-century strong-man Thomas Topham, could snap his fingers while a man danced on each of his outstretched arms.

The Ancient Hebrews were forbidden to eat the flesh of the camel, but to the Persians and Egyptians it was a great delicacy.

St Catherine's Church in Zagreb, Yugoslavia, was constructed in 1632 as a replica of the Church of Jesus in Rome, Italy.

Before the invention of the match, every house used to have its tinder box, a round iron box with tinder (scorched rag) in it, a flint, a piece of steel and a little stick of wood dipped in sulphur.

The shortest reign of any Pope was that of Stephen II who was elected on March 24, 752 and died two days later.

Our sun is about 30,000 light years from the centre of the Milky Way.

The memorial to Mary Washington, mother of George Washington, in Fredericksburg, Virginia, erected in 1894 is the first monument financed by women to honour a woman.

The world's first atomic power station was built at Obinsk, 55 miles south of Moscow, and came into production in 1954.

A former captain of the South Hobart (Tasmania) cricket team took a swipe at a ball and killed a swallow.

Houses were first numbered in Paris in 1463. The practice was adopted in London 300 years later.

The most decorated soldier in World War II was Audie Murphy, the American movie actor.

The first seed-drill was invented by a musician and lawyer, Jethro Tull.

The chemist Dr Adolph von Baeyer (1835–1917) discovered barbituric acid, and named his find not after one of the ingredients, but after his sweetheart, Barbara.

Big Bill Tilden, the tennis player, has hit a tennis ball at 214 km per hour.

The St Edward's crown used in British coronations weighs nearly 5 lbs and contains over 400 precious stones.

Typewriters were first developed to help the blind.

The sandwich owes its name to John Montague, 4th Earl of Sandwich, who, rather than leave the gaming tables, would ask for a slice of meat between two slices of bread.

The bridge of Charenton-le-pont, France, first built in 52 B.C. has been destroyed and rebuilt 17 times.

Our lungs hold from 5 to 8 pints of air.

More people in the United States die in the months of January and February than in any other month. The months with the lowest rate of mortality are July, August and September.

There are thermal areas in New Zealand where, because of the earth's crust being extremely thin, the energy bottled up below the surface bursts through in the form of boiling mud pools.

It is estimated that during the three hundred years of enforced migration to America and the Caribbean more than 20 million Africans were transported there.

The Colosseum in Rome was used for gladiatorial combats and public spectacles for 400 years. It was opened in A.D. 80.

In India camels are still a popular form of transport and in many Indian towns you can see camels 'parked' side by side.

When a ship is overdue or has sunk the 'Lutine' bell in Lloyds of London rings. It gets its name from the British frigate 'Lutine' which sank in 1799 with a cargo worth over three million pounds.

The Jew's Harp has no connection with Jews, but gets its name from the French word 'jou' – meaning a plaything.

The ostrich can run at speeds of up to 40 miles an hour, and on ostrich farms in Cape Province, South Africa, they hold ostrich races for tourists.

Henry Morgan, a notorious pirate, became Lieutenant Governor of Jamaica 1672–1683.

The chronometer which Captain Cook took on his second voyage in 1772 was only 7 minutes 45 seconds slow after three years.

The balloonist, Etienne Montgolfier, designed and launched his first successful balloon in 1793.

In the second half of the nineteenth century policemen had to quell so many riots that a publication suggested they have special uniforms and weapons bristling with sharp spikes.

The most northerly town in the world is in northern Norway, Hammerfest, where the temperature in January is a little below freezing.

In spite of the fact that three-quarters of Greece's total land area is mountainous, rocky and barren, sixty per cent of Greeks make their living from agriculture.

The sun uses an estimated 22 million billion tonnes of hydrogen in a year.

Experts have valued Julius Caesar's autograph at over one million pounds.

A National Atlas of Britain appeared in 1579.

The cigar is named after the Mayan word for smoking, sik'ar.

Henry Montague was made headmaster of Harrow at the age of twenty-six.

The Flying Scotsman has left London for Edinburgh at the same time, 10 a.m., for 100 years, with the exception of the war years, 1939–45, when it left at 9.30.

A Persian wheel is operated by a camel or bullock walking round in circles, to draw water from a well. In Pakistan today there are still 200,000 Persian wells in operation.

Twenty per cent of all Christmas cards sold today are sold in aid of charities.

The British 'X' certificate was introduced in 1951.

In 1889 a Hungarian princess named Anthony Koharry was officially designated a man, as she was the last of her line.

An Indian was pronounced dead in 1886 when both circulation and breathing stopped. As preparations for his funeral were being made, it was found that the man was breathing – and he lived for another 32 years.

Court ladies in fourteenth-century France used to wear their corsets as outer garments.

Over half of all the known types of flowers in the world grow in South Africa.

Mozart, Beethoven and Mendelssohn were all short men.

The body of a hanged man found in Denmark in 1950 was so well preserved that a recent crime was suspected, but it was found that the man had been executed 1000 years ago.

Goethe wrote a story in seven languages when he was barely ten.

Kamchatka Peninsula at the eastern end of the USSR has 20 geysers spurting steam and water, and over 60 active volcanoes.

Before entering a Japanese home, visitors remove their shoes.

Among the organs of a dead ostrich in the London Zoo were found two handkerchiefs, three gloves, a film spool, part of a plastic comb, an alarm clock winding key, part of a rolled gold necklace, two collar studs and a Belgian franc piece.

According to folklore, the Giant's Causeway in Northern Ireland was built by a giant, Finn MacCool. Geologists, however, believe that the odd formation is a result of molten lava going through a process of rapid cooling which caused the lava to crack into these strange formations.

The most dangerous fires for firemen to handle are those where rubber and cork are burning.

Monaco has a greater proportion of the population with telephones than any other country, 965 per 1000 of the population.

The poorest people in the world are the Tasaday tribe of cave-dwellers of central Mindanao, the Philippines, who live without any domesticated animals, agriculture, pottery, wheels or clothes.

Bumping foreheads with a handshake is the traditional greeting in Tibet.

The first parking meters installed were those in Oklahoma City, Oklahoma, in July 1935.

In the United States nearly one quarter of the foods that are produced eventually spoil.

In Japan, social bathing is a relaxing event, and indoor 'pools' are really huge bathtubs.

Male mosquitoes do not bite, only the females.

If you had fifteen books on a shelf and you arranged them in every possible combination, and if you made one change every minute, it would take you 2,487,996 years to do them all.

The cricketer C. B. Fry once hit a ball into the fork of a tree. It was visible, and therefore not a lost ball. By the time they'd got a ladder, he had made sixty-six runs off one ball.

A mouse cannot live in a very cold country as it would lose too much heat from its skin. In a really cold place the smallest mammal is a fox.

The first air charter holiday was organised in 1932 by the Polytechnic Touring Association of London who offered customers a week's holiday in Switzerland for £12–£14.

Robert the Bruce, medieval king of Scotland, was a French aristocrat and a descendant of a Norman lord who had landed with William the Conqueror.

George Bizet famous for his opera, Carmen, was so weakened by rehearsals for its premier, that he died just three months later at the age of 36.

'The' is the most frequently used word in the English language and 'I' is the word most often used in English conversation.

Among the Loango people of Africa, no young man may speak to a girl unless she is in the presence of her mother.

The oldest industry in New York is the fur trade started by the Dutch in 1615.

During the period of their close friendship, Sarah Churchill, the first Duchess of Marlborough, and Queen Anne used to call each other Mrs Freeman and Mrs Morley.

English royalty had only one baptismal name until William III (who was Dutch).

Bands of zinc have been nailed round the bottom of coconut palms in Tahiti. This is to keep rats from climbing into the treetops and eating the coconuts.

There are more than half a million saunas in Finland, and on average Finns take a sauna bath once a week.

In the city of Falun, Sweden, there is a copper mine that has been mined by the same company for more than 700 years.

In the twelfth century Henry I decreed that a yard was to equal the distance from the end of his nose to the end of his thumb.

Apart from bridges and railway lines, Isambard Kingdom Brunel built the first transatlantic wooden paddle-steamer in 1837, and the first iron-hulled screw-propelled steamer, in 1843. When his prototype of the modern ocean liner, the Great Eastern, was launched in 1858 it was six times larger than any other ship afloat.

It was claimed that a tiger shot by Colonel Jim Corbett in 1907 had killed 436 people in India.

All whales, porpoises, dolphins and sturgeon stranded on British shores must be offered to the Queen.

A rattlesnake or viper has special cells between its nostril and its eye which are sensitive to infra-red radiant heat. They can locate people in the dark by the heat they give off.